The Federal Reserve
and the Financial Crisis

THE GEORGE
WASHINGTON
UNIVERSITY

WASHINGTON, DC

In March 2012, the George Washington University offered a course entitled "Reflections on the Federal Reserve and its Place in Today's Economy," featuring Federal Reserve Chairman Dr. Ben Bernanke.

This marked the first university lecture series delivered by a sitting chairman of the Federal Reserve, and provided students in class and online with insights into the nation's central banking system and issues that affect this country and the world.

I am pleased to share with you a compilation of those lectures.

Steven Knapp
President

The Federal Reserve and the Financial Crisis

LECTURES BY

Ben S. Bernanke

PRINCETON UNIVERSITY PRESS

PRINCETON AND OXFORD

Published by Princeton University Press, 41 William Street,
Princeton, New Jersey 08540

In the United Kingdom: Princeton University Press,
6 Oxford Street, Woodstock, Oxfordshire OX20 1TW

Jacket photograph: *Fed Chairman Bernanke Begins Lecture Series at George Washington
University*. Photo: Bloomberg. Courtesy of Getty Images.

press.princeton.edu

Library of Congress Cataloging-in-Publication Data

Bernanke, Ben.

The Federal Reserve and the financial crisis / lectures by Ben S. Bernanke.

pages cm

Includes index.

ISBN 978-0-691-15873-0 (hardcover : alk. paper)
1. United States. Federal Reserve Board. 2. Federal Reserve banks. 3. Global
Financial Crisis, 2008-2009. 4. Financial crises—United States. 5. Monetary policy—
United States. 6. United States—Economic policy—2009- I. Title.

HG2563.B42 2013

330.973'0931—dc23

2012042263

British Library Cataloging-in-Publication Data is available

This book has been composed in Palatino

Printed on acid-free paper. ∞

Printed in the United States of America

3 5 7 9 10 8 6 4

Contents

Publisher's Note

The material in this book was originally delivered as a series of lectures by Ben S. Bernanke at George Washington University in March 2012. This book is taken from the transcript of these lectures, and has been edited for readability. Videos of the lectures and presentation slides are available online at http://www.federalreserve .gov/newsevents/lectures

The Federal Reserve
and the Financial Crisis

Origins and Mission of the Federal Reserve

What I want to talk about in these four lectures is the Federal Reserve and the financial crisis. My thinking about this is conditioned by my experience as an economic historian. When one talks about the issues that occurred over the past few years, I think it makes the most sense to consider them in the broader context of central banking as it has been practiced over the centuries. So, even though I am going to focus in these lectures quite a bit on the financial crisis and how the Fed responded, I need to go back and look at the broader context. As I talk about the Fed, I will talk about the origin and mission of central banks in general; in looking at previous financial crises, most notably the Great Depression, you will see how that mission informed the Fed's actions and decisions.

In this first lecture, I will not touch on the current crisis at all. Instead, I will talk about what central banks are, what they do, and how central banking got started in the United States. I will talk about how the Fed engaged with its first great challenge, the Great Depression of the 1930s. In the second lecture, I will pick up the history from there. I will review developments in central banking and with the Federal Reserve after World War II, talking about the conquest of inflation, the Great Moderation, and other developments that occurred after 1945. But in that lecture I will also spend a good bit of time talking about the buildup to the crisis and some of the factors that led to the crisis of 2008–2009. In lecture three, I will turn to more recent events. I will talk about the intense phase of the financial crisis, its causes, its implications, and particularly the response to the crisis by the Federal Reserve and by other policymakers. And then, in the final lecture I will look at the aftermath. I will talk about the recession that followed the crisis, the policy response of the Fed (including monetary policy), the broader response in terms of the changes in financial regulation, and a little bit of forward-looking discussion about how this experience will change how central banks operate and how the Federal Reserve will operate in the future.

✦ ✦ ✦

So let's talk in general about what a central bank is. If you have some background in economics you know that a central bank is not a regular bank; it is a government agency, and it stands at the center of a country's monetary and financial system. Central banks are very important institutions; they have helped to guide the development of modern financial and monetary systems and they play a major role in economic policy. There have been various arrangements over the years, but today virtually all countries have central banks: the Federal Reserve in the United States, the Bank of Japan, the Bank of Canada, and so on. The main exception is in cases where there is a currency union, where a number of countries collectively share a central bank. By far the most important example of that is the European Central Bank, which is the central bank for seventeen European countries that share the euro as their common currency. But even in that case, each of the participating countries does have its own central bank, which is part of the overall system of the euro.

Central banks are now ubiquitous; even the smallest countries typically have central banks.

What do central banks do? What is their mission? It is convenient to talk about two broad aspects of what central banks do. The first is to try to achieve macroeconomic stability. By that I mean achieving stable growth in the economy, avoiding big swings—recessions and the like—and keeping inflation low and stable. That is the economic function of a central bank. The other function of central banks, which is going to get a lot of attention in these lectures, is to maintain financial stability. Central banks try to keep the financial system working normally and, in particular, they try to either prevent or mitigate financial panics or financial crises.

What are the tools that central banks use to achieve these two broad objectives? In very simple terms, there are basically two sets of tools. On the economic stability side, the main tool is monetary policy. In normal times, for example, the Fed can raise or lower short-term interest rates. It does that by buying and selling securities in the open market. Usually, if the economy is growing too slowly or inflation is falling too low, the Fed can stimulate the economy by lowering interest rates. Lower interest rates feed through to a broad range of other interest rates, which encourages spending on the acquisition of homes, for example, and on construction, investment by firms, and so on. Lower interest rates generate more demand, more spending, and more investment in the economy, and that creates more thrust in growth. And similarly, if the economy is growing too hot, if inflation is becoming a problem, then the normal tool of central bank is to raise interest rates. Raising the overnight interest rate that the Fed charges banks to lend money, known in the United States as the federal funds rate, feeds higher interest rates through the system. This helps to slow the economy by raising the cost of borrowing, of buying a house or a car, or of investing in capital goods, reducing pressure on an overheating economy. Monetary policy is the basic tool that central banks have used for many years to try to keep the economy on a more or less even keel in terms of both growth and inflation.

The main tool of central banks for dealing with financial panics or financial crises is a little less familiar: the provision of liquidity. In order to address financial stability concerns, one thing that central banks can do is make short-term loans to financial institutions. As I will explain, providing short-term credit to financial institutions during a period of panic or crisis can help calm the market, can help stabilize those institutions, and can help mitigate or end a financial crisis. This activity is known as the "lender of last resort" tool. If financial markets are disrupted and financial institutions do not have alternative sources of funding, then the central bank stands ready to serve as the lender of last resort, providing liquidity and thereby helping to stabilize the financial system.

There is a third tool that most central banks (including the Fed) have, which is financial regulation and supervision. Central banks usually play a role in supervising the banking system, assessing the extent of risk in their portfolios, making sure their practices are sound and, in that way, trying to keep the financial system healthy. To the extent that a financial system can be kept healthy and its risk-taking within reasonable bounds, then the chance of a financial crisis occurring in the first place is reduced. This activity is not unique to central banks, however. In the United States, for example, there are a number of different agencies, such as the Federal Deposit Insurance Corporation (FDIC) and the Office of the Comptroller of the Currency, that work with the Fed in supervising the financial system. Because this is not unique to central banks, I will downplay this for the moment and focus on our two principal tools: monetary policy and lender of last resort activities.

Where do central banks come from? One thing people do not appreciate is that central banking is not a new development. It has been around for a very long time. The Swedes set up a central bank in 1668, three and a half centuries ago. The Bank of England was founded in 1694,[1] and was for many decades, if not centuries, the most important and influential central bank in the world. France established a central bank in 1800. So central bank theory and practice is not a new thing. We have been thinking about these issues collectively as an economics profession and in other contexts for many years.

I need to talk a little bit about what a financial panic is. In general, a financial panic is sparked by a loss of confidence in an institution. The best way to explain this is to give a familiar example. If you have seen the movie *It's a Wonderful Life*, you know that one of the problems Jimmy Stewart's character runs into as a banker is a threatened run on his institution. What is a run? Imagine a situation like Jimmy Stewart's, before there was deposit insurance and the FDIC. And imagine you have a bank on the corner, just a regular commercial bank; let's call it the First Bank of Washington, D.C. This bank makes loans to businesses and the like, and it finances itself by taking deposits from the public. These deposits are called demand deposits, which means that depositors can pull out their money anytime they want, which is important because people use deposits for ordinary activities, like shopping.

Now imagine what would happen if, for some reason, a rumor goes around that this bank has made some bad loans and is losing money. As a depositor, you say to yourself, "Well, I don't know if

---

[1] The Bank of England was not set up from scratch as a full-fledged central bank; it was originally a private institution that acquired some of the functions of a central bank, such as issuing money and serving as lender of last resort. But over time, central banks became essentially government institutions, as they all are today.

this rumor is true or not. But what I do know is that if I wait and everybody else pulls out their money and I'm the last person in line, I may end up with nothing." So, what are you going to do? You are going to go to the bank and say, "I'm not sure if this rumor is true or not, but, knowing that everybody else is going to pull their deposits out of the bank, I'm going to pull my money out now." And so, depositors line up to pull out their cash.

Now, no bank holds cash equal to all its deposits; it puts that cash into loans. So the only way the bank can pay off the depositors, once it goes through its minimal cash reserves, is to sell or otherwise dispose of its loans. But it is very hard to sell a commercial loan; it takes time, and you usually have to sell it at a discount. Before a bank even gets around to doing that, depositors are at the door asking, "Where is my money?" So a panic can be a self-fulfilling prophecy, leading the bank to fail; it will have to sell off its assets at a discount price and, ultimately, many depositors might lose money, as happened in the Great Depression.

Panics can be a serious problem. If one bank is having problems, people at the bank next door may begin to worry about problems at their bank. And so, a bank run can lead to widespread bank runs or a banking panic more broadly. Sometimes, pre-FDIC, banks would respond to a panic or a run by refusing to pay out deposits; they would just say, "No more; we're closing the window." So the restriction on the access of depositors to their money was another bad outcome and caused problems for people who had to make a payroll or buy groceries. Many banks would fail and, beyond that, banking panics often spread into other markets; they were often associated with stock market crashes, for example. And all those things together, as you might expect, were bad for the economy.

A financial panic can occur anytime you have an institution that has longer-term illiquid assets—illiquid in the sense that it takes time and effort to sell those loans—and is financed on the other side of the balance sheet by short-term liabilities, such as deposits. Anytime you have that situation, you have the possibility that the people who put their money in the bank may say, "Wait a minute, I don't want to leave my money here; I'm pulling it out," and you have a serious problem for the institution.

So how could the Fed have helped Jimmy Stewart? Remember that central banks act as the lender of last resort. Imagine that Jimmy Stewart is paying out the money to his depositors. He has plenty of good loans, but he cannot change those into cash, and he has people at the door demanding their money immediately. If the Federal Reserve was on the job, Jimmy Stewart could call the local Fed office and say, "Look, I have a whole bunch of good loans that I can offer as collateral; give me a cash loan against this collateral." Then Jimmy Stewart can take the cash from the central bank, pay off his depositors, and then, so long as he really is solvent (that is, as long as his loans really are good), the run will be quelled and the panic will come to an end. So by providing short-term loans and taking collateral (the illiquid assets of the institution), central banks can put money into the system, pay off depositors and short-term lenders, calm the situation, and end the panic.

This was something the Bank of England figured out very early. In fact, a key person in the intellectual development of banking was a journalist named Walter Bagehot, who thought a lot about central banking policy. He had a dictum that during a panic central banks should lend freely to whoever comes to their door; as long as they have collateral, give them money. Central banks need to have collateral to make sure that they get their money back, and that collateral has to be good or it has to be discounted. Also, central banks need to charge a penalty interest rate so that people do not take advantage of the situation; they signal that they really need the money by being willing to pay a slightly higher interest rate. If a central bank follows Bagehot's rule, it can stop financial panics. As a bank or other institution finds that it is losing its funding from depositors or other short-term lenders, it borrows from the central bank. The central bank provides cash loans against collateral. The company then pays off its depositors and things calm down. Without that source of funds, without that lender of last resort activity, many institutions would have to close their doors and could go bankrupt. If they had to sell their assets at fire-sale discount prices, that would create further problems because other banks would also find the value of their assets going down. And so, panic—through fear, rumor, or declining asset values—could spread throughout the banking system. So it is very important to get in there aggressively. As a central banker, provide that short-term liquidity and avert the collapse of the system or at least serious stress on it.

Let's talk a little bit specifically about the United States and the Federal Reserve. The Federal Reserve was founded 1914, and concerns about both macroeconomic stability and financial stability motivated the decision of Congress and President Woodrow Wilson to create it. After the Civil War and into the early 1900s, there was no central bank, so any kind of financial stability functions that could not be performed by the Treasury had to be done privately. There were some interesting examples of private attempts to create lender of last resort functions; for example, the New York Clearing House. The New York Clearing House was a private institution; it was basically a club of ordinary commercial banks in New York City. It was called the Clearing House because, initially, that is what it was; it served as a place where banks could come at the end of each day to clear checks against one another. But over time, clearing houses began to function a little bit like central banks. For example, if one bank came under a lot of pressure, the other banks might come together in the clearing house and lend money to that bank so it could pay its depositors. And so in that respect, they served as a lender of last resort. Sometimes, the clearing houses would all agree that they were going to shut down the banking system for a week in order to look at the bank that was in trouble, evaluate its balance sheet, and determine whether it was in fact a sound bank. If it was, it would reopen and, normally, that would calm things down. So there was some private activity to stabilize the banking system.

In the end, though, these kinds of private arrangements were just not sufficient. They did not have the resources or credibility of an independent central bank. After all, people could always wonder whether the banks were acting in something other than the public interest since they were all private institutions. So it was necessary for the United States to get a lender of last resort that could stop runs on illiquid but still solvent commercial banks.

This was not a hypothetical issue. Financial panics in the United States were a very big problem in the period from the restoration of the gold standard after the Civil War in 1879 through the founding of the Federal Reserve. Figure 1 shows the number of banks closing during each of the six major banking panics during that period in the United States.

You can see that in the very severe financial panic of 1893, more than five hundred banks failed across the country, with significant consequences for the financial system and for the economy. Fewer banks failed in the panic of 1907, but the banks that did fail were larger. After the crisis of 1907, Congress began to think that maybe they needed a government agency that could address the problem of financial panics. A twenty-three-volume study was prepared for the Congress about central banking practices, and Congress moved deliberatively toward creating a central bank. The new central bank was finally established in 1914, after yet another serious financial panic. So financial stability concerns were a major reason that Congress decided to create a central bank in the early twentieth century.

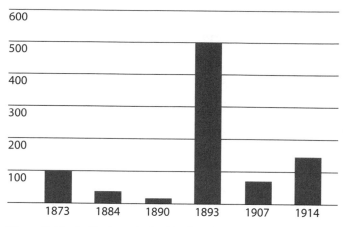

Figure 1. Bank Closings during Banking Panics, 1873–1914
Sources: For 1873–1907, Elmus Wicker, Banking Panics of the Gilded
Age (New York: Cambridge University Press, 2006), table 1.3; for 1914,
Federal Reserve Board, Banking and Monetary Statistics, 1914–1941.

But remember that the other major mission of central banks is
monetary and economic stability. For most of the period from after
the Civil War until the 1930s, the United States was on a gold standard. What is a gold standard? It is a monetary system in which the
value of the currency is fixed in terms of gold; for example, by law
in the early twentieth century, the price of gold was set at $20.67 an
ounce. So there was a fixed relationship between the dollar and a
certain weight of gold, and that in turn helped set the money supply; it helped set the price level in the economy. There were central
banks that helped manage the gold standard, but to a significant
extent a true gold standard creates an automatic monetary system
and is at least a partial alternative to a central bank.

Unfortunately, a gold standard is far from a perfect monetary
system. For instance, it is a big waste of resources: you have to dig
up tons of gold and move it to the basement of the Federal Reserve
Bank in New York. Milton Friedman used to emphasize that a very
serious cost of a gold standard was that all this gold was being dug

up and then put back into another hole. But there are other more serious financial and economic concerns that practical experience has shown to be part of a gold standard.

Take the effect of a gold standard on the money supply. Since the gold standard determines the money supply, there is not much scope for the central bank to use monetary policy to stabilize the economy. In particular, under a gold standard, typically the money supply goes up and interest rates go down in periods of strong economic activity, which is the reverse of what a central bank would normally do today. Because you have a gold standard that ties the money supply to gold, there is no flexibility for the central bank to lower interest rates in a recession or raise interest rates to counter inflation. Some people view that as a benefit of the gold standard—taking away the central bank's discretion—and there is an argument to be made for that, but it does have the side effect that there was more year-to-year volatility in the economy under the gold standard than there has been in modern times. Volatility in output variability and year-to-year movements in inflation were much greater under the gold standard.

There are other concerns with the gold standard. One of the things a gold standard does is to create a system of fixed exchange rates between the currencies of countries that are on the gold standard. For example, in 1900, the value of a dollar was about twenty dollars per ounce of gold. At the same time, the British set their gold standard at roughly four British pounds per ounce of gold. Twenty dollars equals one ounce of gold, and one ounce of gold equals four British pounds, so twenty dollars equals four pounds. Basically, one pound is valued at five dollars. So essentially, if both countries are on the gold standard, the ratio of prices between the two exchange rates is fixed. There is no variability, unlike today, when the euro can go up and down against the dollar. Again, some people would argue that is beneficial, but there is at least one problem: if there are shocks or changes in the money supply in one country and perhaps even a bad set of policies, other countries that are tied to the currency of that country will experience some of the effects.

I will give you a modern example. Today, China ties its currency to the dollar. It has become more flexible lately, but for a long time there has been a close relationship between the Chinese currency and the U.S. dollar. That means that if the Fed lowers interest rates and stimulates the U.S. economy because, say, it is in a recession, essentially monetary policy becomes easier in China as well because interest rates have to be the same in different countries with essentially the same currency. And those low interest rates may not be appropriate for China, and as a result China may experience inflation because it is essentially tied to U.S. monetary policy. So fixed exchange rates between countries tend to transmit both good and bad policies between those countries and take away the independence that individual countries have to manage their own monetary policy.

Yet another issue with the gold standard has to do with speculative attack. Normally, a central bank with a gold standard keeps only a fraction of the gold necessary to back the entire money supply. Indeed, the Bank of England was famous for keeping "a thin film of gold," as John Maynard Keynes called it. The British central bank kept only a small amount of gold and relied on its credibility in standing by the gold standard under all circumstances, so that nobody ever challenged it about that issue. But if, for whatever reason, markets lose confidence in a central bank's commitment to maintain the gold standard, the currency can become subject to a speculative attack. This is what happened to the British. In 1931, for a lot of good reasons, speculators lost confidence that the British pound would maintain its gold convertibility, so (just like a run on the bank) they all brought their pounds to the Bank of England and said, "Give me gold." It did not take very long for the Bank of England to run out of gold because it did not have all the gold it needed to support the money supply, which essentially forced Great Britain to leave the gold standard.

There is a story that while a British Treasury official was taking a bath, an aide came running in saying, "We're off the gold standard! We're off the gold standard!" And the official said, "I didn't know we could do that!" But they could, and they had to. They had no choice because there was a speculative attack on the pound. Moreover, as we saw in the case of the United States, the gold standard was associated with many financial panics. The gold standard did not always assure financial stability.

Finally, one of the strengths that people cite for the gold standard is that it creates a stable value for the currency, it creates a stable inflation. That is true over very long periods. But over shorter periods, maybe up to five or ten years, you can actually have a lot of inflation (rising prices) or deflation (falling prices) with a gold standard because the amount of money in the economy varies according to things like gold strikes. So, for example, if gold is discovered in California and the amount of gold in the economy goes up, that will cause inflation, whereas if the economy is growing faster and there is a shortage of gold, that will cause deflation. So over shorter periods, a country on the gold standard frequently had both inflations and deflations. Over long periods—decades—prices were quite stable.

This was a very significant concern in the United States. In the latter part of the nineteenth century, there was a shortage of gold relative to economic growth, and since there was not enough gold— the money supply was shrinking relative to the economy—the U.S. economy was experiencing deflation, that is, prices were gradually falling over this period. This caused problems, particularly for farmers and people in other agriculture-related occupations. Think about this for a moment. If you are a farmer in Kansas and you have a mortgage that requires a fixed payment of twenty dollars each month, the amount of money you have to pay is fixed. But how do you get the money to pay it? By growing crops and selling them in the market. Now, if you have deflation, that means that the price of your corn or cotton or grain is falling over time, but your payment to the bank stays the same. Deflation created a grinding pressure on farmers as they saw the prices of their products going down while their debt payments remained unchanged. Farmers were squeezed by this decline in their crop prices, and they recognized that this deflation was not an accident. The deflation was being caused by the gold standard.

So William Jennings Bryan ran for president on a platform the principal plank of which was the need to modify the gold standard. In particular, he wanted to add silver to the metallic system so that there would be more money in circulation and more inflation. But he spoke about this in the very eloquent way of nineteenth-century orators. He said, "You shall not press down upon the brow of labor this crown of thorns; you shall not crucify mankind upon a cross of gold." What he was saying is that the gold standard was killing honest, hardworking farmers who were trying to make their payments to the bank and found the price of their crops going down over time.

So the gold standard created problems and was a motivation for the founding of the Federal Reserve. In 1913, finally after all the study, Congress passed the Federal Reserve Act, which established the Federal Reserve. President Wilson viewed this as the most important domestic accomplishment of his presidency. Why did they want a central bank? The Federal Reserve Act called on the newly established Fed to do two things: first, to serve as a lender of last resort and to try to mitigate the panics that banks were experiencing every few years; and second, to manage the gold standard, that is, to take the sharp edges off the gold standard to avoid sharp swings in interest rates and other macroeconomic variables.

Interestingly, the Fed was not the first attempt by Congress to create a central bank. There had been two previous attempts, one

of them suggested by Alexander Hamilton and the second somewhat later in the nineteenth century. In both cases, Congress let the
central bank die. The problem was disagreement between what
today we would call Main Street and Wall Street. The folks on Main
Street—farmers, for example—feared that the central bank would
be mainly an instrument of the moneyed interests in New York and
Philadelphia and would not represent the entire country, would not
be a national central bank. Both the first and the second attempts at
creating a central bank failed for that reason.

Woodrow Wilson tried a different approach: he created not just
a single central bank in Washington but twelve Federal Reserve
banks located in major cities across the country. Figure 2 shows the
twelve Federal Reserve districts (which we still have today), and
each one has a Federal Reserve Bank.[2] Then a Board of Governors
in Washington, D.C., oversees the whole system. The value of this
structure was that it created a central bank where everybody, in
all parts of the country, would have a voice and where information about all aspects of our national economy would be heard in
Washington—and that is, in fact, still the case. When the Fed makes
monetary policy, it takes into account the views of the Federal Reserve banks around the country and thus has a national approach
to making policy.

The Fed was established in 1914 and for a while life was not too
bad. The 1920s, the so-called Roaring Twenties, was a period of
great prosperity in the United States. Its economy was absolutely
dominant in the world at that time because most of Europe was
still in ruins from World War I. There were lots of new inventions.
People gathered around the radio, and automobiles became much
more available. There were a lot of new consumer durables and a

---

[2] Notice, by the way, how many of the little black dots are to the right. In 1914, most of the
economic activity in the United States was in the eastern part of the country. Now, of course,
economic activity is much more evenly spread across the country but the Federal Reserve
banks are in the same locations as in 1914.

Figure 2. Federal Reserve Regions and Locations of Federal Reserve Banks and Board of Governors

lot of economic growth during the 1920s. So the Fed had some time to get its feet wet and establish procedures.

Unfortunately, in 1929 the world was hit by the first great challenge to the Federal Reserve, the Great Depression. The U.S. stock market crashed on October 29th, and the financial crisis of the Great Depression was not just a U.S. phenomenon: it was global. Large financial institutions collapsed in Europe and other parts of the world. Perhaps the most damaging financial collapse was of the large Austrian bank called the Credit-Anstalt in 1931, which brought down many other banks in Europe. The economy contracted very sharply and the Depression lasted for what seems like an incredibly long time, from 1929 until 1941, when the United States entered the war following the attack on Pearl Harbor.

It is important to understand how deep and severe the Depression was. Figure 3 shows the stock market, and you can see at the left a vertical line showing October 1929, a very sharp decline in stock prices. This was the crash that was made famous by many writers including John Kenneth Galbraith and others, who told

Figure 3. S&P Composite Equity Price Index, 1929–1933
Source: Center for Research in Securities Prices, Index File on the S&P 500

colorful stories about brokers jumping out of windows. But what I want you to take from this picture is that the crash of 1929 was only the first step in what was a much more serious decline. You see how stock prices kept falling, and by mid-1932 they had fallen an incredible 85 percent from their peak. So this was much worse than just a couple of bad days in the stock market.

The real economy, the nonfinancial economy, also suffered very greatly. Figure 4a shows growth in real GDP. If the bar is above the zero line, it is a growth period. If it is below, it is a contraction period. In 1929, the economy grew by more than 5 percent and was still growing very substantially. But you can see that from 1930 to 1933, the economy contracted by very large amounts every year. So it was an enormous contraction of GDP, close to one-third overall between 1929 and 1933. At the same time, the economy was experiencing deflation (falling prices). And as you can see in figure 4b, in 1931 and 1932 prices fell by about 10 percent. So if you were a farmer who had had difficulty in the late nineteenth century, imagine what is happening to you in 1932, when crop prices are drop-

(a) **Percent Change**

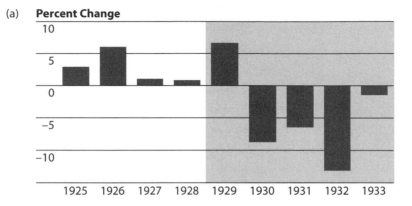

(b) **Percent Change**

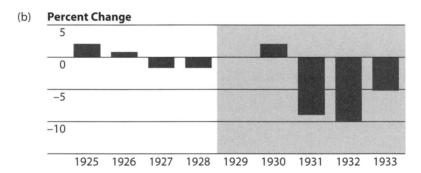

Figure 4a. Real GDP, 1925–1934
Note: Shading represents years of the Great Depression.
Source: Historical Statistics of the United States, Millennial Edition (New York: Cambridge University Press, 2006), table Ca9.

Figure 4b. Consumer Price Index, 1925–1934
Source: Historical Statistics of the United States, Millennial Edition, online, table Cc1.

ping by half or more and you still have to make the same payment to the bank for your mortgage.

As the economy contracted, unemployment soared. We did not have the same survey of individual households in the 1930s that we have today, and so the numbers in figure 5 are estimated; they are not precise numbers. But as best we can tell, at its peak in the early 1930s, unemployment approached 25 percent. The shaded area is

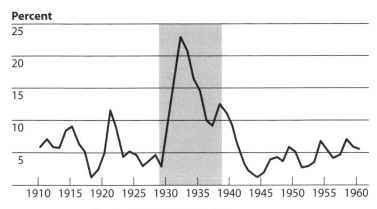

Percent

Figure 5. Unemployment Rate, 1910–1960
Note: Shading represents years of the Great Depression.
Source: Historical Statistics of the United States, Millennial Edition, table Ba475.

the recession period. Even at the end of the 1930s, before the war changed everything, unemployment was still around 13 percent.

As you might guess, with all that was going wrong in the economy, a lot of depositors ran on their banks and many banks failed. Figure 6 shows the number of bank failures in each year, and you can see an enormous spike in the early 1930s.

What caused this colossal calamity (which, I reiterate, was not just a U.S. problem but a global problem)? Germany had a worse depression than the United States, and that led more or less directly to the election of Hitler in 1933. So what happened? What caused the Great Depression? This is a tremendously important subject and has received a lot of attention from economic historians, as you might imagine. And as often is the case for very large events, there were many different causes. A few are the repercussions of World War I; problems with the international gold standard, which was being reconstructed but with a lot of problems after World War I; the famous bubble in stock prices in the late 1920s; and the financial panic that spread throughout the world. So a number of factors caused the Depression. Part of the problem was intellectual—a mat-

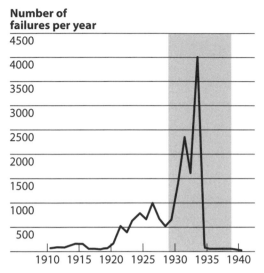

Figure 6. Bank Failures, 1910–1940
Source: Federal Reserve Board, Banking and Monetary Statistics, 1914–1941, table 66

ter of theory rather than policy per se. In the 1930s, there was a lot of support for a way of thinking about the economy called the liquidationist theory, which posited that the 1920s had been too good a time: the economy had expanded too fast; there had been too much growth; too much credit had been extended; stock prices had gone too high. What you need when you have had a period of excess is a period of deflation, a period when all the excesses are squeezed out. This theory held that the Depression was unfortunate but necessary. We had to squeeze out all of the excesses that had accumulated in the economy in the 1920s. There is a famous statement by Andrew Mellon, who was Herbert Hoover's secretary of the Treasury: "Liquidate labor, liquidate stocks, liquidate the farmers, liquidate real estate." It sounds pretty heartless and I think it was, but what he was trying to convey was that we had to get rid of all of the excesses of the 1920s and bring the country back to a more fundamentally sound economy.

What was the Fed doing during this period? Unfortunately, when the Fed confronted its first major challenge in the Great Depression, it failed both on the monetary policy side and on the financial stability side. On a monetary policy side, the Fed did not ease monetary policy as you would expect it to in a period of deep recession, for a variety of reasons: because it wanted to stop stock market speculation, because it wanted to maintain the gold standard, because it believed in the liquidationist theory. And so we did not get the offset to the decline that monetary policy could have provided. And indeed, what we saw was sharply falling prices. You can argue about causes of the decline in output and employment, but when you see 10 percent declines in the price level, you know monetary policy is much too tight. So deflation was an important part of the problem because it bankrupted farmers and others who relied on selling products to pay fixed debts. To make things even worse, as I mentioned earlier, if you have a gold standard, then you have fixed exchange rates. So the Fed's policies were essentially transmitted to other countries, which therefore also essentially came under excessively tight monetary policy and that contributed to the collapse. As I mentioned, one reason the Fed kept money tight was because it was worried about a speculative attack on the dollar. Remember that the British had faced that situation in 1931. The Fed was worried that there would be a similar attack that would drive the dollar off the gold standard. So, to preserve the gold standard, the Fed raised interest rates rather than lower them. They argued that keeping interest rates high would make U.S. investments attractive and prevent money from flowing out of the United States. But that was the wrong thing to do relative to what the economy needed. In 1933, Franklin Roosevelt abandoned the gold standard, and suddenly monetary policy became much less tight and there was a very powerful rebound in the economy in 1933 and 1934.

The other part of the Fed's responsibility is to be lender of last resort. And once again, the Fed did not read its mandate. It responded inadequately to the bank runs, essentially allowing a tremendous decline in the banking system as many banks failed. And as a result, bank failures swept the country. A very large fraction of the nation's banks failed; almost ten thousand banks failed in the 1930s. That continued until deposit insurance was created in 1934. Now, why did the Fed not act more aggressively as lender of last resort? Why didn't it lend to these failing banks? Well, in some cases, the banks were really insolvent. There was not much that could be done to save them. They had made loans in agricultural areas and their loans were all going bad because of the crisis in the agricultural sector. But part of it was the Fed appeared, at least to some extent, to agree with the liquidationist theory, which said that there was too much credit; the country was overbanked; let the system contract; that was the healthy thing to do. But unfortunately, that was not the right prescription.

In 1933, Franklin Roosevelt came to power. Roosevelt had a mandate to do something about the Depression. He took a variety of actions; he was very experimental. Some of those actions were quite unsuccessful. For example, something called the National Recovery Act tried to fight deflation by requiring firms to keep their prices high. But that was not going to help without a bigger money supply. So a lot of things Roosevelt tried did not work, but he did two things that I would argue did a lot to offset the problems the Fed created. The first was the establishment of deposit insurance, the FDIC, in 1934. After that, if you were an ordinary depositor and the bank failed, you still got your money back and therefore there was no incentive to run on the banks. And in fact, once deposit insurance was established, we went from literally thousands of bank failures annually to zero. It was an incredibly effective policy. The other thing FDR did was he abandoned the gold standard. And by abandoning the gold standard, he allowed monetary policy to be released and allowed expansion of the money supply, which ended the deflation and led to a powerful short-term rebound in 1933 and 1934. So the two most successful things that Roosevelt did were essentially offsetting the problems that the Fed created or at least exacerbated by not fulfilling its responsibilities.

So, what are the policy lessons? It was a global depression that had many causes, and the whole story requires you to look at the whole international system. But policy errors in the United States, as well as abroad, did play an important role. And in particular, the Federal Reserve failed in this first challenge in both parts of its mission. It did not use monetary policy aggressively to prevent deflation and the collapse in the economy, so it failed in its economic stability function. And it did not adequately perform its function as lender of last resort, allowing many bank failures and a resulting contraction in credit and also in the money supply. So the Fed did not fulfill its mission in that respect. These are key lessons, and we want to keep these in mind as we consider how the Fed responded to the 2008–2009 financial crisis.

STUDENT: You mentioned the tightening of monetary policy in 1928 and 1929 to stem stock market speculation. Do you think that the Federal Reserve should have taken different actions, such as increasing margin requirements, to stem the speculation or was it wrong for them to take any action at all against the bubble?

CHAIRMAN BERNANKE: That is a good question. The Fed was very concerned about the stock market and believed that it was excessively priced, and there was evidence for that. But they attacked it solely by raising interest rates without paying attention to the effect on the economy. So they wanted to bring down the stock market by raising interest rates, and of course they succeeded! But raising interest rates had major side effects on the economy as well. So, yes, we have learned that asset price bubbles are dangerous and we want to address them if possible, but when you can address them through financial regulatory approaches, that is usually a more pinpoint approach than just raising interest rates for everything. So margin requirements are at least looking at the variety of practices. There were a lot of very risky practices by brokers in the 1920s; it was the equivalent of day traders. Every paper boy had a hot tip for you and there were not many checks and balances on trading, who can make a trade, what margin requirements were, and so on. I think the first line of attack should have been more focused on bank lending, on financial regulation, and on the functioning of the exchanges.

STUDENT: I have a question on the gold standard. Given everything we know about monetary policy now and about the modern economy, why is there still some argument for returning to the gold standard, and is it even possible?

CHAIRMAN BERNANKE: The argument has two parts. One is the desire to maintain "the value of the dollar," that is, to have very long-term price stability. The argument is that paper money is inherently inflationary, but if we had a gold standard we would not have inflation. As I said, that is true to some extent over long periods of time. But on a year-to-year basis it is not true, and so looking at history is helpful there. The other reason advocates want to see a return to the gold standard, I think, is that it removes discretion: it does not allow the central bank to respond with monetary policy, for example to booms and busts, and the advocates of the gold standard say it is better not to give that flexibility to a central bank.

I think, though, that the gold standard would not be feasible for both practical reasons and policy reasons. On the practical side, it is just a simple fact that there is not enough gold to meet the needs of a global gold standard, and obtaining that much gold would cost a lot. But more fundamentally, the world has changed. The reason the Bank of England could maintain the gold standard even though it had very little gold reserves was that everybody knew that the Bank's first, second, third, and fourth priorities were staying on the gold standard and that it had no interest in any other policy objective. But once there was concern that the Bank of England might not be fully commit- ted, then there was a speculative attack that drove it off gold. Now, economic historians argue that after World War I, labor movements became much stronger and there was a lot more concern about unemployment. Before the nineteenth century people did not even measure unemployment, and after World War I you began to get much more attention to unemployment and business cycles. So in the modern world, commitment to the gold standard would mean swearing that under no circum- stances, no matter how bad unemployment got, would we do anything about it using monetary policy. And if investors had 1 percent doubt that we would follow that promise, then they would have an incentive to bring their cash and take out gold, and it would be a self-fulfilling prophecy. We have seen that problem with various kinds of fixed exchange rates that have come under attack during the financial crisis. So I understand the impulse, but if you look at history you will see that the gold standard did not work very well, and it worked particu- larly poorly after World War I. Indeed, there is evidence that the gold standard was one of the main reasons the Depression was so deep and long. And a striking fact is that countries that left the gold standard early and gave themselves flexibility on monetary policy recovered much more quickly than the coun- tries that stayed on gold to the bitter end.

STUDENT: You mentioned that President Roosevelt used deposit insurance to help end bank runs and also abandoned the gold standard to help end deflation. I believe that in 1936 and 1937, up until 1941, we had a double dip and the recession went on. As you have said, today we are sort of out of the recession. What things do you think we need to be careful of—things that possibly were mistakes made in the Great Depression that we should avoid today?

CHAIRMAN BERNANKE: Right, it is not generally appreciated that the Great Depression actually was two recessions. There was a very sharp recession in 1929 to 1933; from 1933 to 1937, there was actually a decent amount of growth and the stock market recovered some; but in 1937 to 1938, there was a second recession that was not quite as serious as the first one but was still serious. There is a lot of controversy about it, but one view that was advanced early on was that the second recession came from a premature tightening of monetary and fiscal policy. In 1937 and 1938, Roosevelt was under a lot of pressure to reduce budget deficits and tighten fiscal policy. The Fed, worried about inflation, tightened monetary policy. I do not want to claim it is that simple—a lot was happening—but the early interpretation was that the reversal in policy was premature, which prevented the recovery from proceeding faster. If you accept that traditional interpretation, you need to be attentive to where the economy is and not move too quickly to reverse the policies that are helping the recovery.

STUDENT: Based on a few of the graphs we saw today and other historical trends, it seems that after an economic slump, recovery often takes five or more years, as represented by the Great Depression and the oil crisis in the 1970s. Do you think it is common for unemployment to remain at high levels until sometimes a half decade after an economic slump, and that criticisms are often premature? And how do you address these concerns in a political environment where short-term fixes rule the day?

CHAIRMAN BERNANKE: Well, the Depression was an extraordinary event. There were many serious declines in economic activity in the nineteenth century, but nothing quite as deep or as long as the Great Depression. The high unemployment that lasted from 1929 until basically World War II was unusual. So we should not conclude that was a normal state of affairs. Now, more generally, some research suggests that following a financial crisis it may take longer for the economy to recover because you need to restore the health of the financial system. Some argue that may be one reason this most recent recovery is not proceeding faster than it is. But I think it is still an open question and there is a lot of discussion about that research. So no, it is not always the case. If you look at recessions in the postwar period in the United States, you see that recoveries very frequently take only a couple of years—recessions are typically followed by a faster recovery. What may be different about this episode—and again this is a subject of debate—is that, unlike the other recessions in the postwar period, this one was related to and triggered by a global financial crisis, and that may be why it is already taking longer for the economy to recover.

STUDENT: Since you said depressions are global recessions, shouldn't there be more global cooperation and shouldn't central banks have a uniform type of fix they cooperate on, instead of every country turning to its own fix?

CHAIRMAN BERNANKE: The Fed and the central banks did cooperate, and continue to cooperate. One of the problems in the Depression was the bad feelings left over from World War I. In the nineteenth century there was a reasonable amount of cooperation among central banks, but in the 1920s, Germany was facing having to pay reparations, and France, England, and the United States were all bickering about war debts, and so the politics was quite bad internationally and that impeded cooperation among the central banks. Also, international central bank cooperation is probably even more important when you have fixed exchange rates. In the 1920s, you had fixed exchange rates because of the gold standard; that meant that monetary policy in one country affected everybody. That was certainly a case for more coordination, but it did not happen. At least today we have flexible exchange rates, which can adjust and tend to insulate other countries from the effects of monetary policy in a given country, so that reduces the need for coordination somewhat—but there is still, I think, a need for coordination.

The Federal Reserve after World War II

It is very helpful to put the recent crisis and the ongoing recovery into historical context. As we go along, I want to make sure you keep your eyes on the ball, that is, the two basic missions of a central bank. The first is maintaining macroeconomic stability: maintaining stable growth and keeping inflation low and stable. The principal policy tool for maintaining macroeconomic stability is monetary policy. In normal times, the Fed and other central banks use open market operations—purchases and sales of securities in markets—to move interest rates up or down, and in doing so try to create a more stable macroeconomic environment.

The second part of a central bank's mission is maintaining financial stability. Central banks are focused on trying to ensure that the financial system functions properly, and in particular, they want to prevent, if possible, and if not, to mitigate the effects of a financial crisis or a financial panic. I talked last time about the lender of last resort function, the notion that in a financial panic, a central bank should follow Bagehot's rule of lending freely against good collateral at a penalty rate, and by providing short-term credit to financial institutions, a central bank can halt or reduce a run or a panic and the accompanying damage to the financial system and the economy.

But let's talk a little bit about history. We left off at World War II, which ended the Depression and led to a sharp drop in unemployment as people were put to work building munitions and serving on the home front. One of the aspects of wars that economists pay attention to is how they get financed. Normally, wars are financed very substantially by borrowing. During World War II, the U.S. national debt increased quite substantially to pay for the war. And the Fed, in cooperation with the Treasury, used its ability to manage interest rates to keep interest rates low, so as to make it cheaper for the government to finance World War II. So that was the role of the Fed during the war.

After the war ended, the debt was still there. The government was still worried about paying the interest on the national debt, which was at a very high level, and so there was considerable pressure on the Fed to keep interest rates low even after the war. But that had the drawback that, if one keeps interest rates low even as an economy is growing and recovering, one risks overheating the economy and triggering inflation. By 1951, the Fed was very concerned about inflation prospects in the United States. After a series of complex negotiations, the Treasury agreed to let the Fed set interest rates independently, as needed, to achieve economic stability. That agreement, called the Fed–Treasury Accord of 1951, was very important because it was the first clear acknowledgment by the government that the Federal Reserve should be allowed to operate independently. Today, around the world there is a very strong consensus that central banks that operate independently will deliver better results than those that are dominated by the government. In particular, a central bank that is independent can ignore short-term political pressures, for example, to pump up the economy before an election, and in doing so, it can take a much longer perspective and get better results. The evidence for this is quite strong. As a result, major central banks around the world are typically independent, which means that they make their decisions irrespective of short-term political pressures.

In the 1950s and the 1960s, the Fed's primary concern was macroeconomic stability. Monetary policy during that period was relatively simple because the economy was growing. As after World War I, the U.S. economy was dominant after World War II. The fears about a renewed Depression had not come true. As a result, a lot of growth was occurring. The Fed tried to follow what is called a "lean against the wind" monetary policy, which means that when the economy is growing quickly (or too quickly), the Fed tightens to try to restrain overheating, and when the economy is growing more slowly, the Fed lowers interest rates and creates some expansionary stimulus in order to avoid a recession. William McChesney Martin, who was chairman of the Federal Reserve from 1951 to 1970, was very attentive to the risks of inflation. He said, "Inflation is a thief in the night." He tried through this "lean against the wind" policy to keep inflation and growth stable. The 1950s were perhaps more tumultuous than you might think, with a serious war in Korea and a couple of recessions during that decade. Nevertheless, it was basically a productive and prosperous decade as the economy went back to civilian operations after the end of World War II.

Things were not to remain completely trouble-free, however. Starting in the mid-1960s, for a variety of reasons that I will discuss, monetary policy became too easy. And after a time when the Fed did not change its policy stance, this easy monetary policy led to a surge in inflation and inflation expectations. Figure 7 shows a graph of inflation. You can see that from 1960 to 1964, inflation averaged only a little over 1 percent per year. It picked up during the Vietnam War period, 1965 to 1969, and went even higher in the early 1970s. By the end of the 1970s, the consumer price index (CPI) inflation rate peaked at about 13 percent. Inflation was a growing problem starting in the mid-1960s and into the 1970s.

Why was monetary policy so easy as to allow inflation to become a problem in the 1970s? One issue was technical: monetary policy-

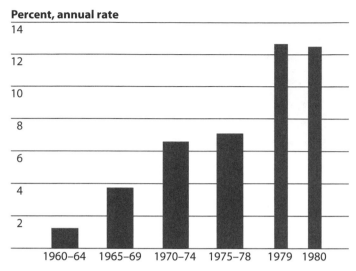

Percent, annual rate

Figure 7. Consumer Price Index (CPI) Inflation, 1960–1964 to 1980
Note: Percentage change calculated from end-of-period to end-of-period.
Source: Bureau of Labor Statistics

makers became too optimistic about how hot the economy could run without generating inflation pressures. It was a general view that unemployment could be kept at a low level, 3 or 4 percent. By keeping inflation a little bit higher, you would be able to get that higher employment level. In the prosperity of the 1950s and the early 1960s, the Fed began to follow that approach. There was actually quite a subtle issue here, which was that economic theory and practice in the 1950s and early 1960s suggested that there was a permanent trade-off between inflation and employment, the notion being that if we could just keep inflation a little bit above normal, we could get permanent increases in employment and permanent reductions in unemployment. That view was taken by many economists during that time.

Milton Friedman, the famous monetary economist, wrote in the mid-1960s quite prophetically that this was going to cause trouble. He argued that an increase in inflation might cause unemployment to fall for a while but at best it would be a transitory effect. The analogy might be to a candy bar: if you eat a candy bar, in the short run it gives you a burst of energy, but after a while, it just makes you fat. Friedman argued, and he turned out to be quite prescient, that attempts to keep unemployment too low through monetary policy were going to end up creating inflation.

Today, it is still debated whether political pressures were put on the Fed to keep monetary policy too easy during that period. After all, this was another period of government deficits, as the government was trying to finance the Vietnam War and the Great Society. That may have influenced the Fed's behavior as well.

You cannot have sustained inflation without monetary policy being too easy. In another famous quote Milton Friedman said, "Inflation is always and everywhere a monetary phenomenon." Nevertheless, a bunch of exacerbating factors made the problem worse and made it more difficult for the Fed to offset the increase in inflation. First, there were a number of shocks to the prices of oil and food. A very striking example occurred in 1973. In October 1973, the Yom Kippur War in the Middle East broke out. In retaliation against U.S. support of Israel, OPEC (Organization of the Petroleum Exporting Countries) used its cartel power to embargo oil exports. Over a short period in the early 1970s, the price of oil almost quadrupled, causing a very sharp increase in gas prices. People were lining up at gas stations to fill their gas tanks. There was a system of even-odd rationing. If your license plate had an even number, you could go to the gas station only on Tuesdays and Thursdays. If it had an odd number, you could go only on Mondays and Wednesdays. It was a very serious issue and there was a lot of unhappiness about gas prices then (as there is today).

Fiscal policy overall was too loose during the late 1960s and early 1970s. The Vietnam War and other government programs increased government spending and increased deficits, which put additional pressure on the capacity of the economy.

Another element that I will mention briefly is wage-price controls. When inflation got up to about 5 percent in the early 1970s, President Richard Nixon introduced wage-price controls, a series of laws that forbade firms from raising their prices. There were exceptions, and there were all kind of boards to try to find exceptions. It was basically a very unsuccessful policy. As you know, prices are the thermostat of an economy. They are the mechanism by which an economy functions. So, putting controls on wages and prices meant that there were shortages and all kinds of other problems throughout the economy. But in addition, as Milton Friedman put it, this was like dealing with an overheating furnace by breaking the thermostat. The fundamental problem was the fact that there was too much aggregate demand driving up prices, and simply passing a law that forbade raising prices did not address the underlying problem of excessive monetary ease and excessive demand. So, wage-price controls kept inflation artificially low for a couple of years, which made it harder for the Fed to figure out what was going on. When the wage-price controls finally collapsed in disarray, because they were creating so many proximity problems in the economy, inflation surged, like a spring that was released. So there were a lot of causes for the increase in inflation.

Arthur Burns, who was the chairman of the Fed during the 1970s, said, "In a rapidly changing world, the opportunities for making mistakes are legion," which is certainly true. One way to think about this whole episode is that after World War II and the end of the Depression, and with the prosperity they saw, economists and policymakers became a little bit too confident about their ability to keep the economy on an even keel. They used the term *fine tuning* to refer to the notion that the Fed and fiscal policy and other government policies could keep the economy more or less perfectly on course and not worry about bumps and wiggles in the economy. That turned out to be too optimistic, too hubristic, as we collectively learned during the 1970s when the efforts of policymakers resulted, not in a lower unemployment rate, which was the original goal, but instead in a very sharp increase in inflation. So one of the themes here is that—and this probably applies in any complex endeavor—a little humility never hurts.

There was a reaction to the increase in inflation in the 1970s, and the key person in this period is Chairman Paul Volcker, who remains to this day an influential figure in economic policy discussions. President Jimmy Carter, whose reelection was seriously threatened by the poor performance of the U.S. economy, appointed Volcker to be the new chairman of the Fed. He did so partly because he thought that Volcker was a tough central banker who would do what was necessary to get inflation under control. And Volcker, who stands six feet eight and smokes a big cigar, certainly gave the impression of somebody who was willing to take strong action. Volcker had been in office for only a few months when he determined that strong action was needed to address the inflation problem. In October 1979, he and the Federal Open Market Committee (FOMC), the policymaking committee of the Fed, instituted a strong break in the way monetary policy was managed. Basically, it allowed the Fed to raise interest rates quite sharply. Raising interest rates slows the economy and brings inflation pressures down. As Volcker said, "To break the inflation cycle, we must have credible and disciplined monetary policy." And it worked. In the years after this program began, inflation fell quite sharply. In figure 8, you can see that from 1980 to 1983, inflation fell from about 12 or 13 percent all the way down to about 3 percent—a relatively quick decline in inflation that offset the problems of the late 1970s. In that respect, the policies of the 1980s were quite successful: they achieved their objective of bringing inflation under control. Nothing is free, however, and one of the effects of these policies was to raise interest rates quite sharply for consumers and businesses. I had just gotten

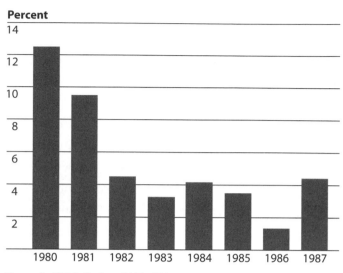

Percent

Figure 8. CPI Inflation, 1980–1987
Note: Percentage change calculated from end-of-period to end-of-period.
Source: Bureau of Labor Statistics

out of graduate school, and I remember in about 1981 or 1982 looking at the possibility of buying a home and being informed that the
rate for a thirty-year mortgage was 18.5 percent. So interest rates
were quite high and, as one might expect, that brought down economic activity and effective inflation as well.

In figure 9, you see the unemployment rate during this period.
The high interest rates, which were necessary to bring down inflation, also caused a very sharp recession. The unemployment rate in
1982 was almost 11 percent, even higher than we saw in the most
recent recession. So, there were definitely very negative side effects
from Volcker's actions.

As you can imagine, the political pressure on the Fed and on
Chairman Volcker was intense. During this period, it was common
practice to mail to the Fed bits of two-by-fours. And on the two-by-
fours it would say, "Stop killing construction," or "Save the farmer,"
or whatever, because the high interest rates were having very nega-

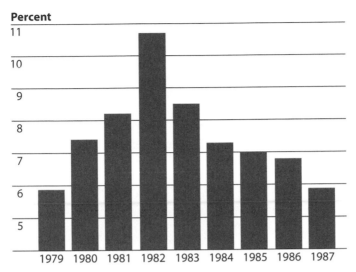

Percent

Figure 9. Unemployment Rate, 1979–1987
Note: Fourth-quarter values.
Source: Bureau of Labor Statistics

tive effects on the economy. I keep a few of these on my desk to remind me that inflation is a concern and that we always have to pay attention to price stability. But this is also an example of why independence is important. If Volcker had needed to be reelected, perhaps he would not have been able to sustain his policy. Instead, he maintained an independent monetary policy. He received at least sufficient support from President Ronald Reagan and from the Congress to be able to carry through the policy, which succeeded in bringing inflation down.

During the 1970s, output and inflation were very volatile. We saw how much inflation moved around. There was a pretty sharp recession in 1973–1975 after the OPEC embargo. And then there was more volatility in the early 1980s as Volcker brought down inflation and the economy went into recession.

Volcker left the chairmanship in 1987, and he was succeeded by Alan Greenspan, who held that position for almost nineteen years, from 1987 to 2006. One of Greenspan's important accomplishments for most of his tenure was achieving greater economic stability. As he said, "an environment of greater economic stability has been key to the impressive growth in the standards of living . . . in the United States." There was so much improvement in the stability of the economy that the period has come to be known as the Great Moderation, as opposed to the Great Stagflation of the 1970s or the Great Depression of the 1930s. The Great Moderation was a very real and striking phenomenon. Figure 10 shows the variability of real GDP growth from 1950 essentially to the present. The line shows quarterly growth rates in GDP. So a sharp peak shows an increase in GDP growth and a drop shows a decline in GDP growth. These are quarterly numbers. You can see the bounciness—periods of rapid growth followed by periods of slower growth. The shaded area in the left-hand portion of the graph is a one standard deviation band. Essentially, it is a measure of the average volatility of GDP growth quarter to quarter during the period between 1950 and 1985. You can see that GDP growth was pretty variable throughout the entire period. There was a lot of volatility in the economy. There were a number of recessions, including the severe ones in 1973 and 1981. Now, look at what happens to GDP variability between 1986 and 2007 or so. The variability from quarter to quarter is much less, and the shaded band to the right shows the average variability of one standard deviation for GDP growth in this latter period. It is very striking how much more stable the economy was over this roughly twenty-year period.

This was true not only for real GDP growth; it was also true for inflation. Figure 11 shows basically the same picture. The vertical line in the middle of the graph splits the time period into pre-1986 and post-1986. The graph shows inflation quarter by quarter as measured by the CPI. Again, the shaded bar on the left side of the graph shows one standard deviation average volatility of inflation

Percent change, annual rate

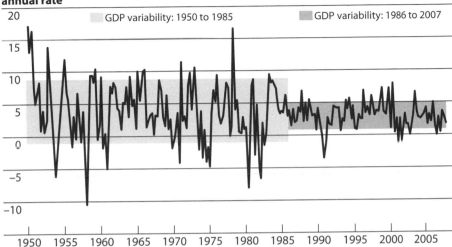

Figure 10. Real GDP Growth, 1950–2010
Note: Data are quarterly. The shaded areas of the graph show plus and minus one standard deviation around the sample period mean of the data, a common measure of data variability.
Source: Bureau of Economic Analysis

Percent change, annual rate

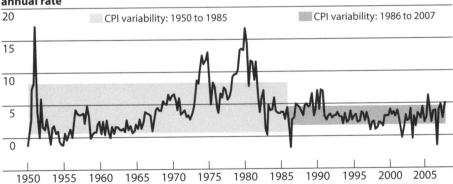

Figure 11. CPI Inflation, 1950–2010
Note: Data are quarterly. The shaded areas of the graph show plus and minus one standard deviation around the sample period mean of the data.
Source: Bureau of Labor Statistics

in the pre-1986 period. You can see the huge spikes in inflation in the 1970s. And then in post-1986, you see much lower volatility. So both growth and inflation were more stable to a quite remarkable extent, which economists commented on quite frequently. That was the so-called Great Moderation.

Why was the economy so much more stable between the mid-1980s and the mid-2000s? Lots of research has been done on this question. There is quite a bit of evidence that monetary policy played a role in creating better stability. In particular, even though Volcker's efforts to bring down inflation in the early 1980s led to a deep recession and a lot of pain in the short term, there was a payoff. That payoff was an economy that was much more stable, with low, stable inflation, more stable monetary policy, and more confidence on the part of business people and households—and that contributed very significantly to broader stability. Remember that Friedman pointed out that there was no long-term trade-off between inflation and unemployment: one could not permanently lower unemployment by keeping inflation a little higher. That is true. But in a different sense, low and stable inflation over a long period makes an economy more stable and supports healthy growth and productivity and economic activity. So low inflation is a very good thing, and the reduction in inflation that occurred in the 1980s was really a global phenomenon. A lot of countries had inflation problems in the 1980s, but all around the world, even developing countries brought down their inflation rates quite considerably, and that has been a positive for economic growth and stability since the mid-1980s.

Not all of the Great Moderation was caused by monetary policy. Other factors no doubt played a role. One is general structural change in the economy. An example would be that, over time, firms have learned how to manage their inventories much more effectively. The practice of so-called just-in-time inventory management is a practice in which, instead of having large stocks of inventory on hand, firms acquire inputs only when they need them for production. Not having large stocks of inventory on hand reduces an important source of fluctuations in the economy because, if demand slows down and you have a big inventory, then you do not do any more production for quite a while until you run down that inventory. Improved management of inventories is just an example (I could cite many others) of better business practices and other factors in the economy that made things more stable. And it may also be the case that there was just better luck—we had fewer oil price shocks and other things happening—and that too may have contributed to the Great Moderation. But as figures 10 and 11 showed, there was quite a striking change in the way the economy operated after the mid-1980s.

Another aspect of the Great Moderation is that there were not any big, damaging financial crises in the United States. There was a stock market crash in 1987, but it did not do much damage. A more significant event was the boom and bust in the dot-com stocks in the late 1990s, and that touched off a mild recession in 2001. But one of the inferences people took away from the Great Moderation was not only was the economy more stable but the financial system seemed more stable as well. As a result, financial stability policies got deemphasized to some extent during this period.

Let's turn now to the prelude to the financial crisis. One of the key events that led ultimately to the recent crisis was a big increase in house prices. Figure 12 shows prices of existing single-family homes, where January 2000 is indexed to be 100. From the late 1990s until early 2006, house prices across the country increased by about 130 percent. You can see that line going straight up, a very sharp increase in home prices. And as I will discuss, at the same time that was happening or perhaps a little bit later in the process, the lending standards for new mortgages to buy homes were deteriorating.

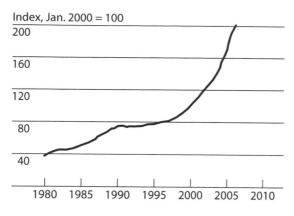

Index, Jan. 2000 = 100

Figure 12. Prices of Existing
Single-Family Houses, 1980–2005
Note: Includes purchase transactions
only.
Source: CoreLogic

Now clearly, a big part of what was happening to create the housing bubble or the increase in housing prices was psychology. After all, the late 1990s was a period with a lot of optimism about tech stocks and the stock market more generally. And some of that optimism, no doubt, spilled over into the housing market. So there was an increasing sense that house prices would keep rising and that housing was a "can't lose" investment. I lived in California for a while, earlier than this but during a period when house prices were rising, and all everybody talked about at cocktail parties was, "What's your house worth now?" and "How much money are you making on your home?" It made working seem rather unnecessary because all you had to do was keep checking the real estate listings. So there was a lot of excitement and enthusiasm about the fact that house prices were going up and making everybody rich. At the same time that this was happening, the standards for underwriting new mortgages were getting worse and worse, which in turn was bringing more and more people into the housing market and pushing up prices even further.

Let's talk a bit about mortgage quality. Prior to the early 2000s, home buyers were typically asked to make a significant down payment of 10 percent, 15 percent, maybe 20 percent of the home price.

And they had to document their finances (their income, their assets, and so on) in great detail to persuade the bank to make them a loan, which in many cases might be four or five times their annual salary. Unfortunately, as house prices rose, many lenders began to offer mortgages to less-qualified borrowers, so-called nonprime mortgages.[3] These mortgages often required little or no down payment and little or no documentation. Essentially, mortgage lenders were moving further down the credit spectrum, lending to more and more people whose credit was less than stellar. You can see this in a number of different ways. Figure 13a shows the percentage of mortgage originations—that is, new mortgages created—that were nonprime (subprime or Alt-A or some other lower-quality mortgage). You can see the very sharp increase, particularly in the middle of the 2000s and 2006. Almost one-third of all mortgages that were originated were nonprime. Figure 13b shows another indicator of the deterioration of mortgage quality: the percentage of nonprime loans with low or no documentation. If you think about it, this is rather perverse. If you are going to make a loan to somebody whose credit is shaky, who does not have a down payment, whose FICO score is low, and so on, one would think you would want to ask them even more questions about their income and their prospects. But, in fact, it went the other way. And as you can see, by 2007, 60 percent of nonprime loans had little or no documentation of the creditworthiness of the borrower. So there was clearly an ongoing deterioration of mortgage quality.

This situation could not go on forever. Figure 14 shows the debt-service ratio. As house prices went up and up and up, the share of borrowers' incomes being spent on their monthly mortgage

---

[3] I say "nonprime" instead of "subprime." Subprime mortgages were the lowest-quality mortgages in terms of the credit of the borrowers, but there were other mortgages that were below the quality of prime mortgages: so-called Alt-A and other types of mortgages. They were also not up to the traditional standards of credit underwriting. So I say "nonprime."

(a) **Percent**

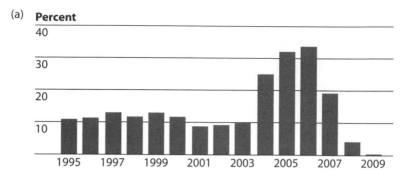

(b) **Percent**

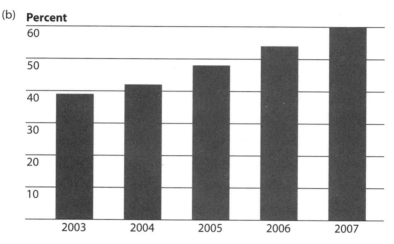

Figure 13a. Nonprime Mortgage Originations (as a Share of Total Originations), 1995–2009
Source: Federal Reserve staff estimates, based on data from Inside Mortgage Finance

Figure 13b. Percentage of Nonprime Loans with Low or No Documentation, 2003–2007
Source: Derived from data in Christopher Mayer, Karen Pence, and Shane M. Sher-
lund, "The Rise in Mortgage Defaults," Journal of Economic Perspectives 23 (winter
2009): 27–50, table 1 and table 2, panel C.

payments went up. As you can see, eventually mortgage payments became quite a large share of personal disposable income,
finally reaching the point that the cost of homeownership was high
enough that it began finally to dampen the demand for new houses.
The debt-service ratio collapsed after that, basically because inter-

**Percent of
disposable income**

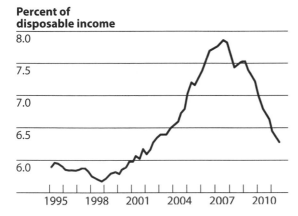

Figure 14. Mortgage Debt-
Service Ratio, 1995–2011
Source: Federal Reserve Board

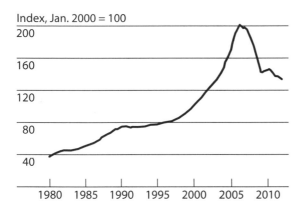

Figure 15. Prices of
Existing Single-Family
Houses, 1980–2010
Note: Includes purchase
transactions only.
Source: CoreLogic

est rates came down. But the main point here is that high payments on mortgages finally meant that there were no longer new home purchasers, and so the bubble burst and house prices fell. Figure 15 shows home prices. You can see the sharp increase from the late 1990s up until about 2006. But from 2006 until today, house prices have fallen more than 30 percent. So there has been a very sharp decline in home prices across the country.

One comment about figure 15: if you look at this graph you might say to yourself, "Oh my gosh, we have a long way to go," because house prices today are still significantly above where they were

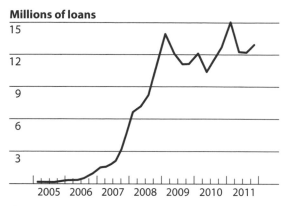

Millions of loans

Figure 16. Mortgages with Negative Equity, 2005–2012
Note: Negative equity number likely is understated because of incomplete data on junior liens.
Source: Federal Reserve staff calculations, based on data from CoreLogic and LPS Applied
Analytics

fifteen years ago. But remember, these prices are in dollar or nominal terms; there is no adjustment for inflation. So even if there was just 2 percent inflation per year, over a period of fifteen years that would raise prices by 30 or 40 percent. So if you adjust for inflation, you find that house prices now are coming much closer to where they were before the beginning of the bubble.

The house price collapse had some significant consequences. One consequence is that many people who had felt rich because their home values had gone up and they had a lot of equity suddenly found themselves underwater, which means that the amount of money they owed on their mortgages was greater than the value of their homes. This is an upside-down situation where the borrower in fact has negative equity in the home. In figure 16, you can see that starting in 2007, the number of mortgages that were in negative equity grew very sharply. Currently, about twelve or thirteen million mortgages out of a total of about fifty-five million or so in the United States—roughly 20 to 25 percent of all mortgages—are currently underwater.

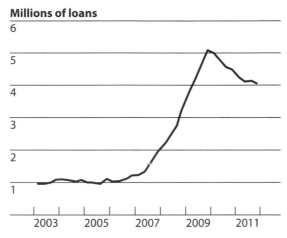

Figure 17. Mortgage Delinquencies, 2003–2012
Note: Loans ninety days or more past due or in foreclosure.
Source: Federal Reserve Board estimates based on data from the MBA National
Delinquency survey

At the same time, given the fact that a lot of people borrowed more than they could afford, the decline in house prices also led to a big increase in mortgage delinquencies, people not paying on time, and ultimately the bank taking over the property—that is called a foreclosure—and then reselling the property to somebody else. Mortgage delinquencies are graphed in figure 17, and you can see that in 2009, there were more than five million mortgages in delinquency, which is almost 10 percent of all mortgages. That is a very, very high rate of delinquencies.

We just looked at the effects of the house price bust on borrowers and homeowners, and those are quite serious. But there is another side to this, which is the effect on lenders. With approximately 10 percent of mortgages in delinquency, banks and other holders of mortgage-related securities suffered sizable losses and that proved to be an important trigger of the crisis. There is an interesting question here. In 1999, 2000, and 2001, we had a big increase in stock prices, including, but not confined to, dot-com or tech bubble prices. Those prices fell very sharply in 2000 and 2001, and a lot of paper wealth was destroyed. In fact, the amount of paper wealth destroyed by the decline in dot-com and other stock prices was not radically different from the amount of wealth destroyed by the bursting of the housing bubble. And yet, the dot-com bust led only to a mild recession. The 2001 recession lasted from March to November 2001; it was only an eight-month recession. Unemployment rose, but not nearly so dramatically as in the 1980s or more recently. And so, here we had a big boom and bust in stock prices, but without causing too much serious or lasting damage to the financial system or the economy. In the recent case, we had a housing boom and bust. If we were looking back at 2001, we would think that would cause a slowdown in the economy, but probably it would not be very serious. That was one of the views we were discussing in the Fed in 2006, as we saw house prices decline. Yet, the decline of house prices had a much bigger impact on the financial system and the economy than the decline of stock prices did. To understand that, it is important to make a distinction between triggers and vulnerabilities. The decline in house prices and the mortgage losses were a trigger. They were a match thrown on kindling. There would not have been a conflagration if there had not been a lot of dry tinder around. In this case, there were vulnerabilities in the economy and in the financial system that the housing bust in some sense set afire. In other words, there were weaknesses in the financial system that transformed what might otherwise have been a modest recession into a much more severe crisis.

What were those vulnerabilities? What was it about the financial system of the United States and of other countries as well that transformed the housing boom and bust into a much more serious crisis? There were vulnerabilities both in the private sector of our financial system and also in the public sector. In the private sector, many borrowers and lenders took on too much debt, too much leverage. And one reason they did that may have been the Great Moderation.

With twenty years of relatively calm economic and financial conditions, people became more confident, willing to take on more debt. The problem with taking on too much debt is that if you do not have much margin, if the value of your asset goes down, then pretty soon you will find that you have an asset that is worth less than the amount of money you borrowed.

A second, very important problem was that during this period, financial transactions were becoming more and more complex but the ability of banks and other financial institutions to monitor and measure and manage those risks was not keeping up. That is, their IT systems and the resources they devoted to risk management were insufficient for them to understand fully what risks they were actually taking and how big the risks were. So if in 2006 you asked a bank about the effect if house prices fell 20 percent, it probably would have greatly underestimated the impact on its balance sheet because it did not have the capacity to measure accurately or completely the risks that it was facing.

A third problem is that financial firms in a variety of contexts relied very heavily on short-term funding such as commercial paper, which can have a duration as short as one day and most of it is less than ninety days. So, like the banks in the nineteenth century that were relying on deposits and making loans, on the liability side of their balance sheets, they had a very short-term, liquid form of liability, which was subject to runs in the same way that deposits were subject to runs in the nineteenth century.

A final private-sector vulnerability was the use of exotic financial instruments, complex derivatives, and so on. An example of this was the credit default swaps (CDSs) employed by the AIG Financial Products Corporation. AIG used CDSs essentially to sell insurance to investors on the complex financial instruments that the investors held. So basically, AIG was promising that if the investor lost any money on collateralized debt obligations or whatever, AIG would make good. As long as the economy and the financial system were doing well, then they were just collecting the premiums on this insurance, essentially, and there was no problem. But once things went bad, their being on one side of all these bets meant that they were exposed to enormous losses, which had, as we will see, very serious consequences. So those are some of the problems that occurred in the private sector.

There were serious problems in the public sector as well. First, the financial regulatory structure was basically the same structure that had been created in the 1930s during the Depression. And in particular, it did not keep up with changes in the structure of the financial system. One aspect of that was that there were many important financial firms that did not really have any serious, comprehensive supervision by any financial regulator. An example was AIG, which was an insurance company. The insurance regulators looked primarily at the insurance products AIG sold. The Office of Thrift Supervision looked primarily at the small banks that AIG owned. But nobody was really looking carefully at this CDS problem that I was just describing. Another category of firms that did not have much oversight was investment banks such as Lehman Brothers and Bear Stearns and Merrill Lynch. There was no statutory oversight of those firms. They had a voluntary agreement with the SEC for oversight, but there really was not comprehensive oversight of those firms. Another group of firms was the government-sponsored enterprises (GSEs) Fannie Mae and Freddie Mac, which did have a regulator but, for reasons I will explain, the regulation was very inadequate. The regulatory structure had lots of holes in it, and there were many firms that proved important during the crisis that did not have good oversight. Even where the law provided for regulation and supervision, it often was not done as well as it should have been.

Although this was true across the whole range of agencies and parts of the government, since I am the Fed chairman, let me talk about the Fed. The Fed made mistakes in supervision and regulation. I would point out two. One would be in its supervision of banks and bank holding companies, it did not press hard enough on this issue of measuring risks. I mentioned earlier that a lot of banks simply did not have the capacity to thoroughly understand the risks they were taking. The supervisor should have pressed them harder to develop that capacity and, if they did not develop that capacity, should have restricted their ability to take risky positions. The Fed and other bank supervisors did not press hard enough on this, and that turned out to be a serious problem. A second area where the Fed performed poorly was in consumer protection. The Fed had authority to provide some protections to mortgage borrowers that, if used effectively, would have reduced at least some of the bad lending that occurred during the latter part of the housing bubble. But for a variety of reasons that was not done to the extent it should have been. In 2007, when I became chairman, we did undertake some of these protections but it was too late to avoid the crisis. So, where there were authorities and powers, they were not always effectively used, and that led to some weaknesses.

A final, and perhaps more subtle, point is that the way our regulatory system is set up, individual agencies, such as the Fed or the Office of the Comptroller of the Currency or the Office of Thrift Supervision, typically had as their responsibility just a specific set of firms. So the Office of Thrift Supervision was responsible only for thrifts and similar institutions. Unfortunately, the problems that arose during the crisis were much broader based than that. They transcended any single firm or small group of firms; they encompassed the whole system. And so essentially what was missing here was enough attention being paid to things that could affect the system as a whole, as opposed to just individual firms. Nobody was in charge of looking to see whether there were problems related to the overall financial system or the relationships among different markets and different firms that could create stress or even a crisis. So those were some of the vulnerabilities in the public sector.

Let me conclude by talking about a controversial topic, the role of monetary policy. Many people have argued that another contributor to the housing bubble was the fact that the Fed kept interest rates low in the early part of the 2000s following the recession of 2001. When the economy got very weak and there was very slow job growth in 2001 and subsequently, and when inflation fell very low, the Fed cut interest rates. In 2003, the federal funds rate got down to 1 percent. There are people who argue that this was one of the reasons that house prices went up as much as they did. And it is true that one of the purposes of low interest rates that the monetary policy achieves is to increase the demand for housing and thereby to strengthen the economy. As I say, this is very controversial. But it is also very important, not only because we want to understand the crisis but also because we want to think about what we should take into account when we formulate monetary policy in the future. To what extent should we be thinking about things like housing bubbles when we make monetary policy?

We have looked at this in great detail inside the Fed, and there has been a lot of research outside the Fed, and (there is no consensus on this and you will probably hear different points of view) the evidence that I have seen suggests that monetary policy did not play an important role in raising house prices during the upswing. Let me talk a little bit about some of the evidence on this question.

One piece of evidence is the international comparison. People do not appreciate that the boom and bust in the United States was not unique. Many countries around the world had booms and busts in house prices, and those booms and busts were not very closely related to the monetary policies of those particular countries. For example, the United Kingdom had a house price boom that was as big or bigger than that in the United States. But monetary policy was much tighter in the United Kingdom than it was in the United States. So there is a puzzle for the monetary theory of the house boom. Another example: Germany and Spain both share the euro, so they have the same central bank, the European Central Bank, and the same monetary policy. Germany's house prices remained absolutely flat throughout the entire crisis, whereas Spain had an enormous house price increase, considerably larger than that in the United States. So the cross-national evidence raises at least some doubts that monetary policy played a large role in the housing bubble.

The second issue is the size of the bubble. It is true that changes in interest rates and mortgage rates should affect house prices and demand for homes. And there is a lot of evidence to look at that over a long period of time. But when you look at how much interest rates changed, including mortgage rates, and how much house prices moved, based on historical relationships, you can explain only a very small part of the increase in house prices. In other words, the increase in house prices was much too large to be explained by the relatively small change in interest rates associated with monetary policy in the early part of the 2000s.

The final piece of evidence I would cite is the timing of the bubble. Robert Shiller, an economist who was well known for his work on bubbles, including the housing bubble, argued that the housing bubble began in 1998, which of course is well before the 2001 recession and before the cut in Federal Reserve interest rates. Moreover, house prices rose very sharply after the tightening began in 2004. So the timing does not line up particularly well. Now, the timing does suggest a couple of other possible explanations. One is that 1998 was right in the middle of the tech boom. And it could be that the same psychological optimism, the same mentality that was feeding stock prices, may have been feeding house prices as well. Another possibility that has been pointed out by a number of economists is that in the late 1990s, there was a very serious financial crisis that hit a number of Asian countries and other emerging-market economies as well. After that crisis was tamed, one response was that many emerging-market countries began to accumulate large amounts of reserves, which meant they had to acquire safe dollar assets. So there was a big increase in the demand for assets, including mortgages. It came from abroad as countries decided they needed to acquire more dollar assets to serve as reserves. Interestingly, probably the strongest correlation across countries that you can find to house price increases is capital inflows, the amount of money coming in to buy mortgages and other assets that were perceived to be safe. That timing would also fit with the beginning in 1998 or so.

So, those are some arguments against the view that monetary policy was an important source of the housing bubble. But I emphasize, economists continue to debate this issue, which is a very important one because, going forward, we have to think about the implications of low interest rates for the economy and the financial system. And in particular, currently, just out of caution, the Fed is doing a lot of financial and regulatory oversight to do the best it can to ensure that nothing is getting unbalanced in the financial system.[4]

What were the consequences of the crisis? The economic consequences were severe. Figure 18 shows a measure of financial stress. It is just an index that combines a variety of financial indicators that indicate that the financial system is under great stress. And you can see what happened in 2008 and 2009: a sharp increase in financial stress in the financial markets. Figure 19 shows that the stock mar-

---

[4] If you want to explore this more, here are a few references on the role of monetary policy in the housing bubble. Ben S. Bernanke, "Monetary Policy and the Housing Bubble," speech delivered at the Annual Meeting of the American Economic Association, Atlanta, January 3, 2010, posted at www.federalreserve.gov/newsevents/speech/bernanke20100103a.htm, summarizes some of the evidence. My speech is based very heavily on Jane Dokko and others, "Monetary Policy and the Housing Bubble," *Economic Policy* 26 (April 2011): 237–287, which presents the results of all the internal Federal Reserve research. Carmen Reinhart and Vincent Reinhart, "Pride Goes before a Fall: Federal Reserve Policy and Asset Markets," NBER Working Paper Series 16815, National Bureau of Economic Research, February 2011, makes the point that interest rates did not move enough to move house prices and also makes the point about capital inflows. Kenneth Kuttner, "Low Interest Rates and Housing Bubbles: Still No Smoking Gun," in Douglas Evanoff, ed., *The Role of Central Banks in Financial Stability: How Has It Changed?* (Hackensack, NJ: World Scientific, forthcoming), concludes that there was no connection between interest rates and the housing bubble. But I emphasize that this question continues to be debated.

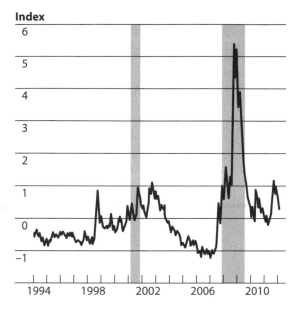

Figure 18. Financial Stress
Index, 1994–2012
Source: St. Louis Federal Reserve
Bank Financial Stress Index

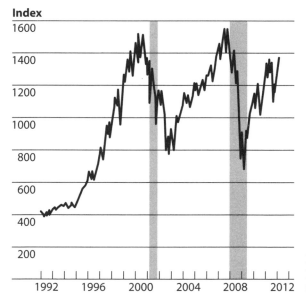

Figure 19. S&P 500 Composite
Index, 1992–2012
Source: Bloomberg

ket plunged. The first decline, in 2000 and the 2001 recession, was a very large decline in tech stocks, but notice that the decline in the stock market in the more recent recession was even bigger than the one in 2000 and 2001. Figure 20 shows home construction. You can see the very sharp decline there. Home construction fell before the recession; of course, it was a trigger of the crisis. But looking to the right, you can see that it still has not really begun to recover. And then finally, figure 21 shows that unemployment rose very sharply, peaked around 10 percent, and has currently fallen to about 8.3 percent.

STUDENT: In the previous lecture, you discussed that in the Depression, it seemed that policy was tightened too early and that led to a double dip. And then today, we were discussing that policy in the 1970s was too slow to tighten. How do we know when the right time is? And is there a right time or does it vary all the time?

CHAIRMAN BERNANKE: It is challenging, and that is certainly one of the reasons that the Fed has so many economists and models and everything to try to figure out what the appropriate moment is to tighten or to ease policy. Forecasting is not very accurate, and so we have to keep looking at what is happening and make adjustments as we go along. The 1970s was particularly difficult because at that time inflation expectations were not at all tied down. If gas prices went up, then people began to expect higher inflation and then to demand higher wages to compensate for the higher prices. And then, of course, higher wages would feed into higher prices, and so on. That was a result of the fact that everybody expected inflation to go up; nobody had any confidence that the Fed or the government in general would keep inflation low and stable. We have a very different situation now, fortunately—and this owes a lot to

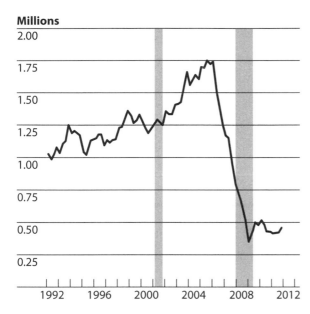

Figure 20. Single-Family
Housing Starts, 1992–2012
Source: Census Bureau

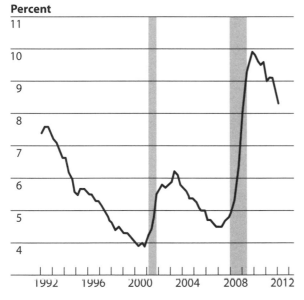

Figure 21. Unemployment
Rate, 1992–2012
Note: Value for the first quarter
of 2012 is the February reading.
Source: Bureau of Labor
Statistics

Chairman Volcker and to Chairman Greenspan as well. After a long period of low inflation, most people are pretty comfortable that inflation will stay reasonably low despite the fact that there are ups and downs with gas prices and so on. That helps a lot because, with inflation staying low, the Fed has more leeway. If policy is easy for a period, that is not necessarily going to feed into a wage-price spiral that would create a much bigger inflation problem down the road. So, keeping inflation expectations low and stable is one of the great accomplishments of Chairman Volcker and Chairman Greenspan, and it is an important objective of central banks around the world.

STUDENT: I have a question about the low interest rate monetary policy in the early 2000s and your view, with all the different research that was conducted, that it did not spark the housing bubble. If you had been Fed chairman in 2001, would you have kept rates that low? Do you think it was the correct thing to do?

CHAIRMAN BERNANKE: I was on the Fed Board during that time and the very first speech I wrote when I became a governor in 2002 was about bubbles and financial supervision and regulation. The theme of my speech was "Use the right tool for the job." The problem with tying interest rate policy to perceived bubbles and asset prices is that it is like using a sledgehammer to kill a mosquito. The problem is that housing is only one part of the economy, whereas interest rates are dedicated to achieving overall economic stability. So we estimate that in order to stop the increase in house prices, interest rates would have had to be raised very dramatically in a period when the economy was very weak. Unemployment was still above normal. Inflation was falling toward zero. And generally speaking, the right way to use monetary policy is to achieve overall macroeconomic stability. Now that does not mean you should ignore financial imbalances. I think the Federal Reserve could have been more aggressive on the supervisory and regulatory side to make sure, for example, that the mortgages being originated were of better quality, that firms were appropriately monitoring their risk, and so on. So I think the first line of defense should be regulation and supervision. One of the lessons I talked about today was not to be too sure of anything, to be humble. For that reason, I think we should never rule out the possibility that, if all of our regulatory and other types of interventions do not achieve the stability and the financial system we want, monetary policy might, as a last resort, be modified to some extent to deal with that problem. But again, because monetary policy is such a blunt tool, which affects all asset prices and affects the entire economy, if you can get a laser-focused type of tool, that is going to be much better for everybody.

STUDENT: At the end of the lecture you mentioned the role that global imbalances played in creating the housing bubble. Doesn't the current U.S. monetary and fiscal policy, which focuses on boosting consumption through borrowing more— doesn't that lead us down the same road of overconsumption through borrowing that got us into the crisis in the first place?

CHAIRMAN BERNANKE: First, we would like to get a better balance in general, so monetary policy stimulates capital formation as well. It also tends to promote exports. So we would like to get a better balance of consumption, investment, and exports, as well as government spending—those are the main components of demand. So current monetary policy is consistent with a better balance. That being said, consumer demand is now far below where it was before the crisis. Consumer spending has not recovered. It is still quite weak relative to where it was before the crisis. Private debt has come down quite a bit. And you mentioned global imbalances, so we are talking about the current account imbalance, or the trade deficit, that the United States has. It has come down quite significantly. So all those things have moved, if anything too far in the short run because we lack a source of demand to keep the economy growing. I agree that every country needs to have an appropriate balance of consumption, capital formation, exports, and government spending, and that is an important task for us. But right now, debt and consumption and so on are still quite low relative to the pattern before the crisis.

STUDENT: The latter part of your lecture was about monetary policy in the 2000s after the dot-com bubble and how interest rates were kept low. You argued that that was not a trigger to the increase in house prices. But to look at it from another point of view, what is your take on the argument that the low interest rates caused private investors and banks to make riskier trades, and that could have been a trigger to the crisis?

CHAIRMAN BERNANKE: That is a good question. I think there is some effect of low interest rates on risk taking. But, once again, it is an issue of getting the right balance. During a recession, generally speaking, on most dimensions, investors become very cautious. That is certainly where they have been for much of the recent past. You want to achieve an appropriate balance between the amount of risk being taken—not too much, not too little—and once again, this is yet another reason why financial supervision and regulation needs to be playing a role. Particularly with large institutions—banks—we need to be looking directly at those firms and making sure that they are managing their risks appropriately. So, again, it is a question of the right tool for the job.

STUDENT: The graphs on the housing bubble show how, clearly, one thing led to another, like rising prices and then eventually a fall. When you were observing the economy in the 2000s, what did you think would happen to the rising house prices in the housing bubble? Did you think that it would eventually lead to a recession? There is a book called *The Big Short* about some investors who were very prescient in shorting the market. What is your take on that?

CHAIRMAN BERNANKE: As I tried to argue, the decline in house prices by itself was not obviously a major threat. In 2005, when I was the chairman of the Council of Economic Advisers for President George W. Bush, we did an analysis for him on what would happen if house prices came down. We concluded that we would have a recession, but we did not anticipate that the decline of house prices would have such a broad-based effect on the stability of the financial system. When I became chairman of the Federal Reserve in 2006, house prices were already declining. In the first two weeks after I became chairman, I gave testimony in which I said: house prices are falling; that is going to have negative impacts on the economy and we are not sure of all the consequences. So we were always aware of the possibility that house prices might come down. The really hard thing to anticipate fully was that the effects of the decline in house prices would be so much more severe than the effects of the somewhat similar decline in dot-com stocks. And again, the reason is the way in which the decline in house prices affected mortgages, which affected the soundness of the financial system and created a panic, which in turn led to the instability of the financial system. So the whole chain of events was critical. It was not just the decline in house prices; it was the whole chain.

STUDENT: Amid the dispersion of cheap credit in the years preceding the housing crisis, there was a bipartisan push for American homeownership, originally spearheaded by President Bill Clinton and later carried on by President George W.

Bush. To what degree could it be argued that that aggressive government policy supporting increased lending during this period contributed to the eventual erosion of credit standards on behalf of the mortgage originators?

CHAIRMAN BERNANKE: That is a very good question, and another controversial one. Certainly, there was some pressure to increase homeownership. There was the American dream aspect of owning a home and so on. Homeownership rose during this period. But to put all the responsibility on the government is probably wrong in this case. Most of the worst loans were made by private-sector lenders and then sold for private-sector securitization, that is, they did not touch Fannie Mae and Freddie Mac. For example, they went directly to investors. Fannie and Freddie did acquire some subprime mortgages, but actually that was a little bit later in the process rather than at the beginning of the process. But clearly the private sector, without any encouragement from the government, was a big player in the decline in mortgage underwriting standards and in the selling of bundled mortgages to private investors.

STUDENT: I think one of the hallmarks of the Fed under your leadership has been your commitment to transparency. All of us in this room are beneficiaries of that policy. But I wonder whether you think too much transparency could actually damage the central bank's credibility, if it gets things wrong.

CHAIRMAN BERNANKE: Generally, I agree that transparency is very important for at least a couple of reasons. I talked already about the importance of a central bank being independent. So there is one linkage there. But if a central bank is independent and making important decisions that affect everybody, then it has to be accountable. People have to understand what it is doing, why it is doing it, and on what basis it makes its decisions. So for democratic accountability, I think it is important for the central bank to be transparent. I testify all the time, I give speeches, I have town hall meetings and other kinds of meetings like this, I give press conferences, and I think it is very important for me to explain what the Fed is doing and why it is doing it. The other reason for transparency is that, over time, there has been increased understanding that most of the time, transparency can make monetary policy work better. So, for example, if the Federal Reserve communicates that its future actions will be X or Y and conveys that information to the markets, the markets may respond by building those expectations into interest rates, which may have a more powerful effect in the economy. So communication also reduces uncertainty and helps increase the impact of monetary policy in financial markets.

STUDENT: My question concerns price stability and inflation expectations. You mentioned the importance of macroeconomic stability and long-run economic growth. Given the massive amount of liquidity that has been pumped into the market recently, how has the Fed been able to keep inflation expectations so low?

CHAIRMAN BERNANKE: I think we owe something to my predecessors—Chairman Volcker, in particular, and also Chairman Greenspan—who got inflation down low and kept it there. People get used to what they see. And in a world in which inflation remains low year after year, people become more and more confident that the central bank—the Fed or whoever—will meet its mandate of keeping inflation low. It has been very striking that, even though we have had movements in oil prices and other shocks to the economy, deep recession and financial crisis, throughout most of the period inflation expectations have been very well tied down to about the 2 percent range that the Fed is trying to hit.

The Federal Reserve's Response to the Financial Crisis

Today I want to talk about the Federal Reserve's response to the financial crisis. In the last couple of lectures I mentioned a key theme, the two main responsibilities of central banks—financial stability and economic stability. Let me turn it around and talk about the two main tools. For financial stability, the main tool the central banks have is lender of last resort powers by providing short-term liquidity to financial institutions, replacing lost funding. Central banks, as they have for a number of centuries, can help calm a financial panic. For economic stability, the principal tool is monetary policy; in normal times, that involves adjusting short-term interest rates.

Today I will discuss the intense phase of the financial crisis in 2008 and 2009, and so I will focus primarily on the lender of last resort function of the central bank. I will come back to monetary policy in the final lecture when we talk about the aftermath and recovery.

Last time I talked about some of the vulnerabilities in the financial system that transformed into a crisis the decline in housing prices, which by itself seemed no more threatening than the decline in dot-com stock prices. Because of these vulnerabilities, the decline in housing prices led to a very severe crisis. The vulnerabilities I talked about last time were private-sector vulnerabilities, including the excessive debt taken on perhaps because of the period of the Great Moderation; very important, the banks' inability to monitor their own risks; excessive reliance on short-term funding (which, as a nineteenth-century bank would tell you, makes it vulnerable to a run as short-term funding is pulled away); and increased use of exotic financial instruments such as credit default swaps and others that concentrated risk in particular companies or in particular markets. Those were the vulnerabilities in the private sector.

The public sector had its own vulnerabilities, including gaps in the regulatory structure. Important firms and markets did not have adequate oversight. Where there was adequate oversight, at least by law, sometimes the supervisors and regulators did not do a good enough job. For example, not enough attention was paid to forcing banks to do a better job of monitoring and managing their risks. And finally, an important gap we have really begun to look at since the crisis is that, with individual agencies looking at different parts of the system, not enough attention was being paid to the stability of the financial system as a whole.

Let me talk for a moment about another important public-sector vulnerability, the so-called government-sponsored enterprises (GSEs) Fannie Mae and Freddie Mac. Fannie Mae and Freddie Mac are nominally private corporations (they have shareholders and a board) but they were established by Congress in support of the housing industry. Fannie and Freddie, as they are called, do not make mortgages. You cannot go to Fannie's headquarters and get a mortgage. Instead, they are the middleman between the originator of the mortgage and the ultimate holder of the mortgage. If you are a bank and you make a mortgage loan, if you like you can sell the mortgage to Fannie or Freddie. They will, in turn, take all the mortgages they purchase and put them together into mortgage-backed securities (MBSs) to sell to investors. A mortgage-backed security is just a security that is a combination of hundreds or thousands of underlying mortgages. That process is called securitization. Fannie and Freddie pioneered this basic approach to getting funding from mortgages. In particular, when the GSEs, Fannie and Freddie, sell their mortgage-backed securities, they provide guarantees against credit loss. So if the underlying mortgages in those MBSs go bad, Fannie and Freddie make the investor whole. Now, Fannie and Freddie were permitted to operate with inadequate capital. So they were particularly at risk in a situation with a lot of mortgage losses. They did not have enough capital to make good on their guarantees. Although many aspects of the financial crisis were not anticipated, this one was. Going back for at least a decade before the crisis, the Fed and many other people said that Fannie and Freddie just did not have enough capital and that they were a danger to the stability of the financial system. What made the situation even worse was that Fannie and Freddie, besides selling mortgage-backed securities to investors, also purchased on their own account large amounts of mortgage-backed securities, both their own and some that were issued by the private sector. They made profits from holding those mortgages but, to the extent that those mortgages were not insured or protected, Fannie and Freddie were vulnerable to losses and, without adequate capital, they were at risk.

It was not just the house price boom and bust but also the mortgage products and practices that went along with the house price movements that were particularly damaging and that were important triggers of the crisis. There were a lot of exotic mortgages, by which I mean nonstandard mortgages (standard mortgages are thirty-year prime fixed-rate mortgages). All different other kinds of mortgages were being offered, often to people with weaker credit. One feature that many of these mortgages shared was that, in order for them to be repaid, house prices had to keep increasing. For example, you might be a borrower who would get an adjustable-rate mortgage (ARM), where the initial interest rate was 1 percent, which meant that you could afford the payment for the first year or two. Now, after two years, the mortgage interest rate might go up to 3 percent, then after four years, 5 percent, and then higher and higher. In order to avoid that, at some point you would have to refinance into a more standard mortgage. As long as house prices were going up, creating equity for homeowners, it was possible to refinance. But once home prices stopped rising—and by 2006 they were already declining quite sharply—rather than having built equity, borrowers found themselves underwater. They could not refinance and found themselves stuck with increasing payments on their mortgages.

Some examples of bad mortgage practices include:

- interest-only (IO) adjustable-rate mortgages (ARMs);
- option ARMs (which permit borrowers to vary the size of monthly payments);
- long amortizations (payment periods greater than thirty years);
- negative amortization ARMs (initial payments do not even cover interest costs); and
- no-documentation loans.

Most of these bad mortgage practices shared the feature that they reduced monthly payments early in the mortgage but allowed mortgage payments to rise over time. Take, for example, an option ARM, which is an adjustable-rate mortgage with the option for borrowers to vary how much they pay. They could pay less than the full amount owed each month and what they did not pay just got rolled back into the mortgage. The other common feature of bad mortgage practices, such as no-doc loans, was that there was very little underwriting, which means very little analysis to make sure that the borrower was creditworthy and was able to make the payments on the mortgage.

Figure 22. The Deterioration of Lending Practices

Figure 22 shows two advertisements from the period that can illustrate some of the issues. I like the one on the right. We removed the name of the company. Let's look at the features it is offering. A "1 percent low start rate": the start rate is what you pay the first year; it does not tell you about the next year. "Stated income" means that you tell the company what your income is, and they write it down; that is all the checking they do. "No documentation" is self-explanatory. A "100 percent finance" means that no down payment is required. "Interest-only loans" means that you pay the interest but you do not have to pay any principle back. And "debt consolidation" is an interesting arrangement that allows you to go to the mortgage company and say, "Well, not only do I want to borrow money to buy the house, but also I want to add in all my credit card debt and everything else I owe, and put that into one big mortgage payment, and I'll pay for that with the 1 percent start rate." Obviously, these are some very problematic practices.

Mortgage companies, banks, savings and loans, and a variety of other institutions originated these nonprime mortgages, but where did these mortgages wind up? How were they financed? Some of them were kept on the balance sheet of the mortgage originator, but many or even most of these exotic or subprime mortgages were packaged in securities and sold off into the market.

Some mortgage-backed securities were relatively simple. If the mortgages were sold to Fannie and Freddie, they had to meet Fannie and Freddie's underwriting standards. Fannie and Freddie would combine them into mortgage-backed securities and sell them with a guarantee, as I discussed. Those are relatively simple securities made up of basically just hundreds or thousands of underlying mortgages.

But some of the securities that were being created were very complex and very hard to understand. An example would be a collateralized debt obligation (CDO). This would often be a security that combines mortgages and other types of debt together in one package. And it could be sliced in different ways so that one investor could buy the safest part of the security and another investor could buy the riskiest part. These securities were very complicated and required a lot of analysis.

One reason that many investors were willing to buy these securities was because they had the reassurance that the rating agencies, whose job is to rate the quality of bonds and other securities, gave triple-A ratings to many of these securities—essentially saying that these securities were very safe and one did not have to worry about their credit risk. Many of these securities were sold to investors, including pension funds, insurance companies, foreign banks, and even, in some cases, wealthy individuals. But the financial institutions that created these securities often retained some of them as well. For example, sometimes they would create an accounting fiction, an off-balance-sheet vehicle, which would hold these securi-

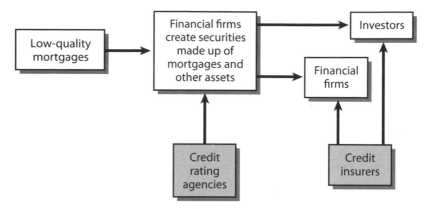

Figure 23. Subprime Mortgage Securitization

ties and finance itself using cheap short-term funding such as commercial paper. So, some of the securities went to investors and some of them stayed with the financial institutions themselves.

In addition, we had companies, such as AIG, that were selling insurance. They were using various kinds of credit derivatives to say, "Pay us a premium and if the mortgages in your mortgage-backed security go bad, we will make you whole." That makes the security triple-A rated. Of course, these practices made the underlying securities no better, and basically they created a situation where risks could be spread throughout the system.

Figure 23 is a diagram showing how a subprime mortgage securitization might work. On the left, where the box reads "low-quality mortgages," you might have a mortgage company or a thrift company making loans. This thrift or mortgage company does not care too much about the quality of the loan because the company is going to sell it anyway. So they sell the mortgages to large financial firms, which in turn take those mortgages, and maybe other securities as well, and combine them into a security that is essentially an amalgamation of all the underlying mortgages and other securities.

Now, the financial firm that created the security might negotiate with the credit-rating agency, asking, "What do we have to do to get a triple-A rating?" There would be negotiations and discussion and, in the end, the security would be rated triple-A. The financial firm could then cut up the security in different ways or sell it as is to investors such as pension funds. But again, financial firms kept many of these securities on their own books or in related investment vehicles. And finally, on the right in the figure, you have credit insurers such as AIG and other mortgage insurance companies that for a fee provided insurance in case the underlying mortgages went bad. So this is the basic structure of the securitization process. I have seen complete flowcharts and they are incredibly complex. This is a very simplified version, but the basic idea is there.

As you recall, a financial crisis or panic occurs when you have any kind of financial institution that has illiquid assets (long-term loans, for example) but liquid short-term liabilities (deposits, for example). In a classic bank panic, if bank depositors lose faith in the quality of the assets held by the bank, they run and pull out their money; the bank cannot pay off everybody because it cannot change their loans into cash fast enough; and so the run on the bank is self-fulfilling. The bank will either fail or have to dump all of its long-term assets quickly in the market and take big losses.

The crisis of 2008–2009 was a classic financial panic but in a different institutional setting: not in a bank setting but in a broader financial market setting. As house prices fell in 2006 and 2007, for the reasons I described, people who had subprime mortgages were not able to make the payments. It was increasingly evident that more and more were going to be delinquent or default, and that was going to impose losses on the financial firms, the investment vehicles they had created, and also on credit insurers like AIG. Unfortunately, the securities were extremely complex and financial firms' monitoring of their own risks was not sufficiently strong. The problem was not just the losses. If you put together all the subprime mortgages in the United States and assumed they were all worthless, the total losses to the financial system would be about equivalent to one bad day in the stock market: they were not very big. The problem was that they were distributed throughout different securities and different places and nobody really knew where they were and who was going to bear the losses. So that created a lot of uncertainty in the financial markets.

As a result, wherever you had short-term funding, whether commercial paper or other types of short-term funding, the lenders refused to lend. We had all kinds of funding that was not deposit insured; it was so-called wholesale funding, which came from investors and other financial firms. Whenever there was doubt about a firm, as in a standard bank run, the investors, the lenders, and the counterparties would all pull back their money quickly for the same reason that depositors would pull their money out of a bank that was thought to be having trouble. So there was a whole series of runs, which generated huge pressures on key financial firms as they lost their funding and were forced to sell their assets quickly, and many important financial markets were badly disrupted. During the Depression, thousands of banks failed, but almost all of them, at least in the United States, were small banks (some larger banks failed in Europe). The difference in 2008 was, in addition to the many small banks that failed, there were also intense pressures on quite a few of the largest financial institutions in the United States.

Let's look at some of the firms that came under intense pressure. Bear Stearns, a broker-dealer, came under intense pressure in the short-term funding markets in March 2008 and was sold to JPMorgan Chase with Fed assistance on March 16. Things calmed down a bit after that, and over the summer there was some hope that the financial crisis would moderate. But then in the late summer, things really began to pick up.

On September 7, 2008, Fannie and Freddie clearly were insolvent. They did not have enough capital to pay the losses on their mortgage guarantees. The Federal Reserve worked with Fannie and

Freddie's regulator and with the Treasury to determine the size of the shortfall, and over that weekend, the Treasury with the Fed's assistance placed those firms into a form of limited bankruptcy called a conservatorship. At the same time, the Treasury got authorization from Congress to guarantee all of Fannie and Freddie's obligations. So, the firms were in a partial bankruptcy but the U.S. government now guaranteed their mortgage-backed securities. So that protected those investors. That had to be done or else it would have been an enormous intensification of the crisis because investors all over the world held literally hundreds of billions of dollars' worth of those securities.

In the middle of September, Lehman Brothers, a broker-dealer, had severe losses. It came under great pressure and could not find anybody either to buy it or to provide it with capital. And so on September 15th, it filed for bankruptcy. On the same day, Merrill Lynch, another big broker-dealer, was acquired by the Bank of America, basically saving the firm from potential collapse.

The next day, on September 16th, AIG, the largest multidimensional insurance company in the world, which had been selling credit insurance, came under enormous attack from people demanding cash either through margin requirements or through short-term funding. The Fed provided emergency liquidity assistance for AIG and prevented the firm from failing.

Washington Mutual was one of the biggest thrift companies, a big provider of subprime mortgages. It was closed by regulators on September 25th. After parts of the company were split off, JPMorgan Chase acquired this company as well. On October 3rd, Wachovia, one of the five biggest banks in the United States, came under serious pressure and was acquired by Wells Fargo, another large mortgage provider.

All the firms I am talking about were among the top ten or fifteen financial firms in the United States, and similar things were happening in Europe. So, this was not a situation where only small banks were affected. Here we had the largest, most complex international financial institutions on the brink of failure.

Let's review the lessons from the Great Depression, which I discussed in the first lecture. First, the Fed did not do enough to stabilize the banking system in the 1930s, and so the lesson there is that in a financial panic, the central bank has to lend freely, according to Bagehot's principle, to halt runs and to try to stabilize the financial system. Second, the Fed did not do enough to prevent deflation and contraction of the money supply in the 1930s, so the second lesson from the Great Depression is that you need to have accommodative monetary policy to help the economy avoid a deep recession. So, heeding those lessons, the Federal Reserve and the federal government took vigorous actions to stop the financial panic, working domestically with other agencies and internationally with foreign central banks and governments.

Now, one aspect of the crisis that, I think, does not receive enough attention is that it was global. In particular, Europe as well as the United States was suffering very severely from the crisis. But it was also a very impressive example of international cooperation.

On October 10, 2008, as it happened, there was a previously scheduled meeting in Washington of the G7 industrial countries, the seven largest industrial countries, and the central bank governors and the finance ministers of those seven countries met in Washington. Now, I will tell you a deep, dark secret: these big, high-profile international meetings are usually a terrible bore because much of the work is done in advance by the staff. We have a discussion, but the communiqué has already been written by the staff and in most cases what happens at the meeting is fairly routine. This was not one of those boring meetings. We essentially tore up the agenda and discussed what we should do. How should we work together to stop this crisis that was threatening the global financial system? In the end we came up with a statement of principles that was written from scratch, based on some Fed proposals. Among those principles were that we would work together to prevent the failure of any more systemically important financial institutions. This was after Lehman Brothers had failed. We would make sure that banks and other financial institutions had access to funding from central banks and capital from governments. We would work to restore depositor confidence and investor confidence, and then we would cooperate as much as possible to normalize credit markets. This was a global agreement, and the following week, the United Kingdom was the first to announce a comprehensive program to stabilize its banking system. The United States announced major steps to put capital into our banks, and so on. So a lot happened in the next couple of days after this meeting.

To show you how effectively this worked, figure 24 graphs the interest rate charged on overnight loans between banks, the interbank interest rate. Normally, the overnight interest rate between banks is extremely low, far less than 1 percent, because banks need some place to park their money overnight and they have a lot of confidence that it is safe to lend to another large bank overnight. As you can see, starting in 2007 banks lost confidence in one another, which is shown by the increase in the rates they charged one another to make loans. For example, in 2007, you begin to see the pressures as house prices began to fall and there were increasing concerns about the quality of mortgage securities and the financial soundness of firms. In March 2008, you can see another little peak around the time Bear Stearns was forced to sell itself. That does not look like much, in comparison to what happened later, but that was a very difficult period. It was a period of quite sharp movements in financial markets and in funding markets. Now, look what happened in response to Bear Stearns's liquidity problems. There was an enormous spike in interbank market rates, and probably not

Basis points

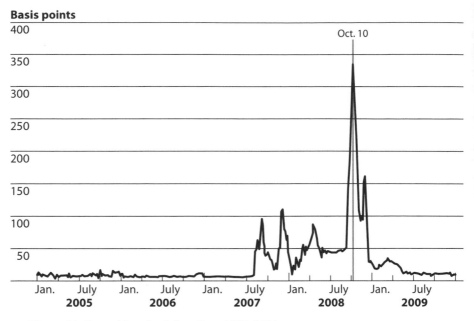

Figure 24. Cost of Interbank Lending, 2005–2009
Note: London Interbank Offered Rate (LIBOR) minus overnight index swap rate
Source: Bloomberg

much lending was taking place even at those high rates. This indi-
cated that suddenly there was no trust whatsoever even between
the largest financial institutions because nobody knew who was
going to be next, who was going to fail, who was going to come
under funding pressure.

Look what happened after the international announcements.
Within a few days we began to see a reduction in funding pressure,
and by early January there was an enormous improvement in the
funding pressures in the banking system. This is a great example of
international cooperation and it illustrates the point that this was
not just a U.S. phenomenon, it was not just U.S. policy, it was not
just the Federal Reserve. It really was a global cooperative effort,
particularly between the United States and Europe.

The Fed played an important role, however, in providing liquidity, in making sure that the panic was controlled. I will talk briefly

about this in general and then I will present two case studies that will illustrate some of the issues. The Federal Reserve has a facility called the discount window, which it uses routinely to provide short-term funding to banks, maybe a bank that finds itself short of funding at the end of the day. It wants to borrow overnight. It has collateral with the Fed. Based on that collateral, it can borrow overnight at the discount rate, which is the interest rate the Fed charges. So the discount window, which allows the Fed to lend to banks, is always operative. No extraordinary steps were needed to lend to banks. The Fed always lends to banks. We did make some modifications in order to reassure banks about the availability of credit. And to get more liquidity into the system, we extended the maturity of discount window loans, which were normally overnight loans. We made them longer-term and we had auctions of discount window funds, in which firms bid on how much interest they would pay. The idea there was by having a fixed amount that we were auctioning, we would at least assure ourselves that we got a lot of cash into the system. The point here is that the discount window, which is the Fed's usual lender of last resort facility lending to banks, was operative and we used it aggressively to make sure that the banks had access to cash to try to calm the panic.

But our financial system is a lot more complicated than the one that existed when the Fed was created in 1913. We have many different kinds of financial institutions in markets now. And as I said, the crisis was like an old-fashioned bank crisis, but it happened to all different kinds of firms and in different institutional contexts. So the Fed had to go beyond the discount window. We had to create a whole bunch of other programs, special liquidity and credit facilities that allowed us to make loans to other kinds of financial institutions, on the Bagehot principle that providing liquidity to firms that are suffering from loss of funding is the best way to calm a panic. All these loans were secured by collateral. We were not taking chances with taxpayers' money. But the cash was going not just to banks but also more broadly into the system. Again, the purpose of this was to enhance the stability of the financial system and get credit flows moving again. Let me emphasize that this is the traditional lender of last resort function of central banks that has been around for hundreds of years. What was different was that it took place in a different institutional context than just the traditional banking context.

Here are some of the institutions and markets that we addressed through our special programs. Banks were covered by the discount window. But another class of financial institutions, broker-dealers (financial firms that deal in securities and derivatives), were also facing very serious problems. They included Bear Stearns, Lehman Brothers, Merrill Lynch, Goldman Sachs, Morgan Stanley, and others. The Fed provided cash or short-term lending to those firms on a collateralized basis as well. Commercial paper borrowers received assistance, as did money market funds. In the modern financial system, not just mortgages but also auto loans, credit cards, and all different kinds of consumer credit are funded through the securitization process. For example, a bank might take all of its credit card receivables, bundle them together into a security, and then sell them in the market to investors, much as mortgages are sold, and that is called the asset-backed securities market. The asset-backed securities market essentially dried up during the crisis, and the Fed created some new liquidity programs to help get it started again, which we were successful in doing.

I should mention that although the Fed's lending to banks was totally standard lending through the normal discount window, these other types of lending required the Fed to invoke emergency authority. There is a clause, 13(3), in the Federal Reserve Act that says that under unusual and exigent circumstances (basically, in an emergency), the Fed can lend to entities other than just banks. This authority had not been used by the Fed since the 1930s. But in this particular case, with all these other problems emerging in different institutions and in different markets, we invoked this authority and used it to help stabilize a variety of different markets.

Let me give you a case study that will help you understand what we did and how it helped the economy. I want to talk a little bit here about money market funds. Money market funds are basically investment funds in which you can buy shares, and the funds take your money and invest it in short-term liquid assets. Money market funds historically almost always maintain a one-dollar share price. So they are very much like a bank, and they are often used by institutional investors such as pension funds. A pension fund with thirty million dollars in cash probably would not put that into a bank because that much money is not insured; there is a limit to how much deposit insurance covers.

So what a pension fund might do instead of putting the cash in a bank would be to put the money into a money market fund, which promises one dollar for each dollar put in, plus a little bit of interest on top, and invests in very short-term, safe, liquid assets. So it is a reasonably good way to manage your cash if you are an institutional investor.

As I said, money market shares do not have deposit insurance, but the investors who put their money into a money market fund expect that they can take their money out at any time, dollar for dollar. So they treat it like a bank account, basically. The money market funds in turn have to invest in something, and they tend to invest in short-term assets such as commercial paper. Commercial paper is a short-term debt instrument issued typically by corporations, short-term in that its maturity is ninety days or less. A nonfinancial corporation might issue commercial paper to allow it to manage its cash flow. It might need some short-term money to meet its payroll or to cover its inventories. So ordinary manufacturing companies such as GM or Caterpillar would issue commercial paper to get cash to manage their daily operations. Financial corporations,

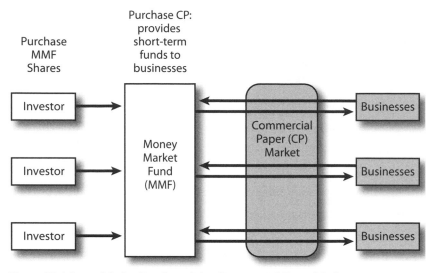

Figure 25. Money Market Funds and the Commercial Paper Market

including banks, would also issue commercial paper to get funds that they could then use to manage their liquidity positions and to make loans to the private economy. Figure 25 is a diagram of how a money market fund works. On the left, you see investors investing their excess cash in the money market fund. The money market fund buys commercial paper, which is basically a funding source for both nonfinancial businesses, such as manufacturers, and for financial companies that would lend it to other borrowers.

What happened to this arrangement during the 2008 crisis? Lehman Brothers created a huge shock wave. It was an investment bank, a global financial services firm; it was not a bank, so it was not overseen by the Fed. It held lots of securities and it did a lot of business in the securities markets. It could not take deposits, not being a bank. Instead, it funded itself in short-term funding markets, including the commercial paper market. Lehman invested heavily in mortgage-related securities and also in commercial real estate during the 2000s. As house prices fell and delinquencies on mortgages rose, Lehman's financial position got worse and it was also losing lots of money on its commercial real estate investments. So Lehman was becoming insolvent, it was losing money on all of its investments, and it was coming under a lot of pressure. And indeed, as Lehman's creditors lost confidence, they started withdrawing funding from Lehman. For example, investors refused to roll over Lehman's commercial paper and other business partners said, "Well, we're not going to do business with you anymore because we're afraid you're not going to be here next week." So Lehman was losing money and increasingly unable to fund itself. It tried with the help of the Federal Reserve and the Treasury to find somebody willing either to put more capital into the firm or to acquire the firm. It was unable to do that, so on September 15th, as I mentioned, it filed for bankruptcy. This was an enormous shock that affected the whole global financial system.

One of the many effects of the failure of Lehman Brothers was on money market funds. One particular fairly large money market fund held, among its other assets, commercial paper issued by Lehman. When Lehman failed, that commercial paper became either worthless or at least completely illiquid for a long time. Suddenly, this money market fund could no longer pay off its depositors at a dollar per share. It didn't, and it lost money. Now, suppose you are an investor in a money market fund and you know that if you ask for your dollar back, you can get it. But you also know that the fund does not have enough cash to pay everybody a dollar. What are you going to do? The same thing nineteenth-century bank depositors would do if they heard that their bank had lost money. So, investors in this fund and then in other money market funds began to pull out their money, just like a standard bank run. We had a very intense bank run or, in this case, a money market fund run, in which investors in these funds began to pull out their money just as quickly as they could.

Billions of dollars (daily)

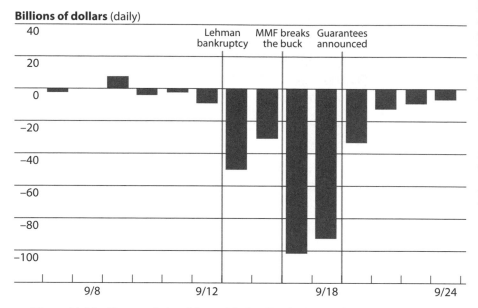

Figure 26. Net Flows to Prime Money Market Funds, September 7–24, 2008
Source: iMoneyNet and Federal Reserve Board staff adjustments

The Fed and the Treasury responded very quickly to the situation. The Treasury provided a temporary guarantee that investors would get their money back if they did not pull it out right then. And the Fed created a backstop liquidity program, under which it lent money to banks, which in turn used that money to buy some of the assets of the money market funds. That gave the money market funds the liquidity they needed to pay off their depositors and helped to calm the panic.

To give you a sense of what was happening, figure 26 shows the daily money outflows from the money market funds. This is a two-trillion-dollar industry. You see the Lehman bankruptcy, and a couple of days later you see the money market fund breaking the buck, which meant that it was unable to pay its investors a dollar a share. Following that announcement, you can see that for two days, about one hundred billion dollars a day was flowing out of these funds. Within two days, the Treasury announced the guarantee program and the Fed came in to support the liquidity of these funds. And as you can see, the run ended pretty quickly. This was an absolutely classic bank run and a classic response: providing liquidity to help the institution being run provide cash to its investors, and providing guarantees. That successfully ended the run.

But that was not the end of the story, because the money market funds were also holding commercial paper. And as they began to face runs, they in turn began to dump commercial paper as quickly as they could. As a result, the commercial paper market went into shock. This is an excellent example of how financial crises can spread in all different directions. Lehman failed. That, in turn, caused the money market funds to experience a run, which led to a shock in the commercial paper market. So, everything is connected to everything else and it is really hard to keep the system stable. As the money market funds withdrew from the commercial paper market, there was a sharp increase in rates in the commercial paper market, and lenders were not willing to lend for more than maybe one day to commercial paper borrowers, which in turn affected the ability of those companies to function and the ability of those financial institutions to fund themselves.

Once again, the Federal Reserve, responding in the way Bagehot would have had it respond, established special programs. Basically, it stood as a backstop lender; it said: "Make your loans to these companies, and we will be here ready to backstop you if there is a problem rolling over these funds." That restored confidence in the commercial paper market.

Figure 27 shows commercial paper rates. Once again, you can see the panic phenomenon, a sharp increase in rates, which really understates the pressure because it does not include the fact that for many companies, they could not get funding at any interest rate. Or if they got funding, it was only for overnight or very short-term periods. The Fed's actions restored confidence in that market, and you can see the response: rates came back down at the beginning of 2009.

Basis points
(5-day moving average)

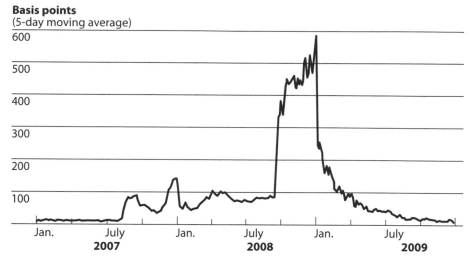

Figure 27. Cost of Short-Term Borrowing, 2007–2009
Note: Spread between the A2/P2 nonfinancial rate and the AA nonfinancial rate
Source: Depository Trust & Clearing Corporation

A lot of what I have been discussing you probably did not read too much about in the newspapers. I was working with these critical markets and providing broad-based liquidity to financial institutions to try to bring the panic under control. But the Fed and the Treasury also got involved in trying to address problems with some individual critical institutions.

In March 2008, as I mentioned, a Fed loan facilitated the takeover of Bear Stearns by JPMorgan Chase, avoiding a failure of that firm. The reasons we undertook that action were, first, at the time the financial markets were quite stressed and we were fearful that the collapse of Bear Stearns would greatly add to that stress and perhaps set off a full-fledged financial panic; and second, we judged that Bear Stearns was solvent. At least JPMorgan Chase thought so; it was willing to buy the firm and to guarantee its obligations. So by lending to Bear Stearns, the Fed was acting consistent with the proposition that it should make loans that are likely to be paid back. The Fed felt that it was well secured in making that loan.

In the second example, AIG was very close to failure in October 2008. AIG, again, was the world's largest insurance company. It was a complicated company. It was a multinational financial services company with many constituent parts, including a number of global insurance companies. But part of the company, called AIG Financial Products, was involved in all kinds of exotic derivatives and other types of financial activities, including, as I mentioned, the credit insurance that it was selling to the owners of mortgage-backed securities. So when the mortgage-backed securities started going bad, it became evident that AIG was in big trouble and its counterparties began demanding cash or refusing to fund AIG, and it came under tremendous pressure.

In our estimation, the failure of AIG would have been basically the end. It was interacting with so many different firms. It was so interconnected with both the U.S. and the European financial systems and global banks. We were quite concerned that if AIG went bankrupt, we would not be able to control the crisis any further. Now, fortunately, from the perspective of lender of last resort theory, although AIG was taking a lot of losses in its financial products division, underlying those losses was the world's largest insurance company. So AIG had lots and lots of perfectly good assets. Therefore, it had collateral that it could offer to the Fed to allow us to make a loan to provide the liquidity it needed to stay afloat.

And so, to prevent the collapse of AIG, we used AIG assets as collateral and loaned AIG eighty-five billion dollars. Later, the Treasury provided additional assistance to keep AIG afloat. That was highly controversial. The action was legitimate, we thought, first in terms of lender of last resort theory because it was a collateralized loan—and the Fed has in fact been fully paid back—and second, because AIG was a critical element in the global financial system. Over time AIG stabilized. It has repaid the Fed with interest. The Treasury still owns a majority of its stock, but AIG has been paying back the Treasury as well.

I would like to emphasize that what we had to do with Bear Stearns and AIG is obviously not a recipe for future crisis management. First, it was a very difficult and, in many ways, distasteful intervention that we had to do to prevent the system from collapsing. But clearly, there is something fundamentally wrong with a system in which some companies are "too big to fail." If a company is so big that it knows that it is going to get bailed out, that is not at all fair to other companies. But even beyond that, "too big to fail" gives these big companies an incentive to take excessive risks, where they will say: "Well, we'll take big risks. Heads I win, tails you lose. If the risks pay off, we make plenty of money. And if they don't pay off, the government will save us." That is a situation that we cannot tolerate.

So, the problem we had in September 2008 was we really did not have any tool—legal tools or policy tools—that allowed us to let Bear Stearns and AIG and the other firms go bankrupt in a way that would not cause incredible damage to the rest of the system. And therefore we chose the lesser of two evils and prevented AIG from failing. That being said, we want to be sure that this never happens again. We want to be sure that the system is changed so that if a large systemically critical firm like AIG comes under this kind of pressure in the future, there will be a safe way to let it fail, so that it can fail and the consequences of its mistakes can be borne by its management and shareholders and creditors without bringing down the whole financial system.

Finally, let me say a few words about the consequences of the crisis. We did stop the meltdown. We avoided what would have been, I think, a collapse of the global financial system. That was obviously a good thing. But one thing that I was always sure of and the Federal Reserve was always sure of was that a collapse of some of these big financial firms was going to have very serious collateral consequences. There were people arguing even as late as September 2008, "Well, why don't you just let the firms collapse? There is a system that can take care of it: bankruptcy. Why don't you let them fail?" We never thought that was a good option. Particularly, if the whole system had collapsed, we would have had extraordinarily serious consequences.

As it was, even though we prevented a total meltdown, there were still very serious collateral impacts not just on the U.S. economy but on the global economy as well. So following the crisis, even though the crisis was brought under control, the U.S. economy and much of the global economy went into a sharp recession. U.S. GDP fell by more than 5 percent, which is quite a deep recession. Eight and a half million people lost their jobs and unemployment rose to 10 percent.

And, as I said, this was not just a U.S. situation. The U.S. recession was, in fact, a rather average recession. Many countries around the world had worse declines, particularly those dependent on international trade. So it was a global slowdown. And as all this was happening, fears of another Great Depression were very real. Nevertheless, the Great Depression was much worse than the recent recession. And I think the view is increasingly gaining acceptance that without the forceful policy response that stabilized the financial system in 2008 and early 2009, we could have had a much worse outcome in the economy.

I will close with a couple of indicators to compare the recent recession with the Great Depression. First, figure 28 shows the stock market. The darker line starts in August 1929, which was the peak of the stock market before the Great Depression. The lighter line shows the more recent stock prices, starting in October 2007. And then each of the graphs shows you the evolution of stock prices in the Depression period and in the more recent period. What is striking is that for the first fifteen or sixteen months, stock prices in the United States behaved in this crisis very much as they did in 1929 and 1930. But about fifteen or sixteen months into the recent crisis, in early 2009, about the time that the financial crisis was stabilizing, look what happened. In the Depression era, stock prices kept fall-

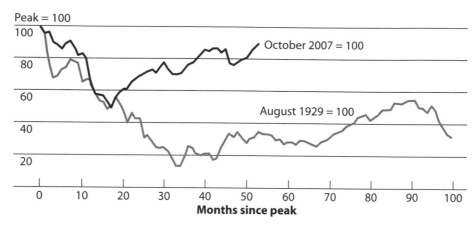

Figure 28. S&P 500 Composite Index for Up to 95 Months since Peak, 1929 versus 2007

ing and, as I mentioned, in the end stock prices lost 85 percent of their value. In the recent crisis, by contrast, U.S. stock prices recovered and began a long recovery, and they now are more than double where they were three years ago.

Figure 29 shows industrial production, a measure of output. Again, the lighter line graphs the more recent data. The darker line graphs the Depression-era data. You can see that in this recent crisis the fall in industrial production was not quite as severe or as fast as in the Depression. But you get the same basic phenomenon that about fifteen to sixteen months into the episode, about the time that the financial crisis was brought under control, industrial production bottomed out and began a period of steady recovery, whereas in the Depression, the collapse continued for several more years.

STUDENT: In both this lecture and the previous one, you mentioned the increasing issuance of exotic and subprime mortgages. Why are financial institutions willing to bear so much risk to lend even to borrowers with poor credit? And if they had foreseen the decreasing prices in the housing market, would they still have made those loans?

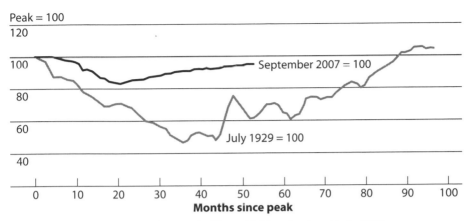

Figure 29. Industrial Production for Up to 95 Months since Peak, 1929
versus 2007
Source: Federal Reserve Board

CHAIRMAN BERNANKE: There were a couple of reasons. One was simply the fact that firms were probably too confident about house price increases and said, "Well, house prices are likely to keep rising." And in a world in which house prices are rising, these are not such bad products because people can afford to pay for a year but then they can refinance to something more stable, and this may be a way to get people into housing. But the risk was that house prices would not keep rising, and of course that is ultimately what happened.

The second reason was that the demand for securitized products grew very substantially during this period. In part, there was a large international demand from Europe and from Asia for high-quality assets, and always-clever U.S. financial firms figured out that they could take a variety of different kinds of underlying assets, whether subprime mortgages or whatever, and through the miracle of financial engineering they could create from them at least some securities that would be rated triple-A, which they could then sell abroad to other investors. Unfortunately, that sometimes left them with the remaining bad pieces, which they kept or sold to some other financial firm.

So there were trends in the financial markets, including overconfidence about their ability to manage those risks; a belief that house prices would probably keep rising; a sense that after they made those mortgages, they could sell them to somebody else and that other investor would be willing to acquire them; a big demand for "safe assets." For all those reasons, it was actually a very profitable activity while it lasted. It was only when house prices began to fall that it became a big loser.

STUDENT: You were talking about how one of the major things the Fed had to do was figure out how to get liquidity flowing again in the market. That reminds me of the Volcker Rule because, as I understand it, the Volcker Rule bans proprietary trading by investment banks, but it also left gray areas for principal trades, which, as I understand, are very important for market makers to create markets and find liquidity. So I wonder what you think about that. Doesn't that seem rather counterintuitive?

CHAIRMAN BERNANKE: Well, the Volcker Rule is a part of the Dodd-Frank financial regulatory reform, which the Fed and other agencies are tasked with implementing. The purpose of the Volcker Rule, as you said, is to reduce the risk of financial institutions by preventing banks and their affiliates from doing proprietary trading, which means doing short-term trading on their own accounts.

The Dodd-Frank law recognizes that there are legitimate reasons that banks might want to acquire short-term securities and it makes certain exceptions for them. They include, for example, hedging against risk. But one particular exception is to make markets, to serve as intermediaries who buy and sell in order to create liquidity in a particular market—that is exempted from the Volcker Rule. One of the challenges of implementing this rule is trying to figure out how to create a set of standards that allows the so-called exempted or legitimate activities, such as market making and hedging, while ruling out proprietary trading. That is very difficult, and we are working on that. We put out a rule and we have gotten thousands of comments, which we are looking at to figure out how best to do that.

But the point you raised is that liquidity in markets is important. During the crisis, it was a much worse problem than just a lack of trading volume. You had big financial institutions unable to find the funding to support their asset positions, which left them with two possibilities: either defaulting because they do not have enough funding, or (the tack that many of them took) selling off assets as quickly as possible, which in turn spreads panic. Because if there is a huge seller's market for, say, commercial real estate bonds, that is going to drive the price down very sharply. And then any company that is holding those bonds finds its financial position being eroded and that creates pressure on it.

I did not use the word *contagion* in my discussion. A contagion, just as in an illness context, is the spreading of panic, the spreading of fear from one market or institution to another. Contagion has been a major problem in many financial panics, and certainly in this one. That was one of the mechanisms that caused funding pressures to jump from firm to firm and created such a broad-based problem.

STUDENT: I have a question about global collaboration during the financial crisis. You talked about the G7 in 2008. Specifically, as we saw multinational corporations begin to be on the brink of failure, what pressures came from the international community when the decision to, say, bail out AIG was being debated?

CHAIRMAN BERNANKE: Well, there weren't any real pressures. Everything was happening too fast. I think one area where collaboration was not as good as we would like was in dealing with some of these multinational firms. For example, there were problems between the United Kingdom and the United States over the failure of Lehman Brothers, and inconsistencies that caused problems for some of Lehman's creditors.

So one of the things we are trying to do under the Dodd-Frank financial reform legislation, as I mentioned before, is to create provisions for safely allowing large financial firms to fail. But one of the complexities is that many of the firms that this would be applied to are multinational firms, operating not just in two or three countries but maybe in dozens of countries. And so, we are collaborating with other countries in figuring out how we would work together to help a large multinational firm fail as safely as possible. We tried during the crisis to cooperate in mostly ad hoc ways, and we were in touch with regulators in the United Kingdom and elsewhere. But, given the time frame and the lack of preparation, we did not do as much as we would have been able to do with more lead time. So I think that was a weakness of international collaboration.

For the most part, though, countries cooperated in dealing with the financial institutions that were based in their own countries. AIG was an American company, and we dealt with that, whereas Dexia, which was a European company, was dealt with by the Europeans. Also, there was a lot of cooperation between central banks. A lot of European banks needed dollar funding as opposed to euro funding. They use dollar funding because they hold dollar assets and they make loans to support trade, which is often done in dollars, so they needed dollars. The European Central Bank cannot provide dollars. So we did what was called a swap, where we gave the European Central

Bank dollars and they gave us euros. They took the dollars we gave them and lent them on their own recognizance to European banks, easing dollar funding pressures around the world. So, those swaps, which are still in existence because of the recent issues in Europe, were an important example of collaboration. Also, in October 2008, right as this crisis was intensifying, the Federal Reserve and five other central banks all announced interest rate cuts on the same day. So we coordinated even our monetary policy. There were some areas, such as multinational firms, where a lot more preparation was needed and we are still working on those things cooperatively today.

STUDENT: Could you elaborate on the off-balance-sheet vehicles that were being used and why banks were allowed to keep that much information off their books?

CHAIRMAN BERNANKE: It has to do with accounting rules, basically. You create this separate vehicle, and the bank might have substantial interest in that vehicle. It might, for example, have a partial ownership. It might have some promises to provide credit support if it goes bad or liquidity support if it needs cash. But under the rules that existed at that time, if the amount of control that the bank had on this off-balance-sheet vehicle was sufficiently limited, then according to the accounting rules, the bank could treat it as a separate organization, not part of the bank's own balance sheet. That allowed the banks to get away with holding somewhat less capital reserves, for example, than they would have had to carry if all these assets were on their own balance sheets.

One of the many good developments since the crisis is that these rules have been reworked, and many of the off-balance-sheet vehicles that existed before the crisis would no longer be allowed. They would have to be consolidated, which means they would have to be made part of the bank's balance sheet, have appropriate capital reserves, and so on. So those practices are not completely gone, but the accounting rules have greatly tightened the situations and circumstances under which a bank can put something off its balance sheet into a separate investment vehicle.

STUDENT: You mentioned several large firms that came under pressure in 2008 and also the Fed's doctrine, if you will, of "too big to fail." Where do you draw the line between bailing out a bank and allowing it to fail? Is it arbitrary or is there some sort of methodology that the Fed goes by?

CHAIRMAN BERNANKE: This is a great question. First, I want to resist the word *doctrine*. These firms proved to be too big to fail in the context of a global financial crisis. That was a judgment we made at the time based on their size, their complexity, their interconnectedness, and so on. It was not something that we ever thought was a good thing. Again, one of the main goals of the financial reform is to get rid of "too big to fail" because it is bad for the system. It is bad for the firms. It is unfair in many ways, and it would be a great accomplishment to get rid of "too big to fail." So it was not something that we advocated or supported in any way. We were just in a situation where we were forced to choose the least bad of a number of different options.

During the crisis, we had to make judgments on a case-by-case basis, and we were trying to be as conservative as possible. In the case of AIG, there was really not much doubt in our minds. This was a case where action was necessary, if at all possible. Lehman Brothers was itself probably "too big to fail," in the sense that its failure had enormous negative impacts on the global financial system. But there we were helpless because it was essentially an insolvent firm. It did not have enough collateral to borrow from the Fed. We cannot put capital into a firm that is insolvent. This was before the Troubled Asset Relief Program (TARP), which provided capital that the Treasury could use. So we had no legal way to save Lehman Brothers. I think if we could have avoided letting it fail, we would have done so. In the two cases where we intervened, Bear Stearns and AIG, the judgment was pretty clear, given not only the firms themselves but also the environment at the time.

Now interestingly, we have had to get much more into this issue since the crisis because there are a number of different rules and regulations that actually require the Fed and other regulatory agencies to make some determination about how systemically critical a firm is. For example, the new Basel 3 capital requirements require the largest, most systemically critical firms to have a capital surcharge. They have to hold more capital than firms that are not as systemically critical. As part of that process, the international bank regulators have worked together to set up criteria relating to size, complexity, interconnectedness, derivatives, and a whole bunch of other criteria that help determine how much extra capital these large firms have to hold. Likewise, the Fed, when it considers a proposed merger of two banks, now has to evaluate whether the merger would create a systemically more dangerous situation. So we have worked hard, and we have put out a variety of criteria including some numerical thresholds that we look at to try to figure out if a merger creates a systemically critical firm, and if it does, we are not supposed to allow that merger to happen.

So, the science of doing this is progressing. It is still in its infancy. But we are looking very seriously at this and, indeed, now that the Fed has become much more focused on financial stability, we have a whole division of people working on various metrics and indicators to try to identify risks to the system and firms that need to be particularly carefully supervised and maybe required to hold extra capital because of the potential risk they pose to the system.

STUDENT: One vulnerability that you mentioned was that the credit-rating agencies were assigning triple-A ratings to securities that carried much more risk than perhaps a triple-A rating might warrant. It seems as though the incentives would be aligned for the buyers to seek out ratings that were more accurate because they would be taking on more risk. Was there a systemic problem as far as how incentives were aligned within the credit-ratings system that allowed these faulty ratings to propagate throughout the system?

CHAIRMAN BERNANKE: Yes, there were some incentive problems, and you identify one of them, which is that, instead of the seller of the security being the one who hires and pays the credit rater, you would think that it would be in the interest of the buyers, who after all are the ones bearing the risk, to band together and pay the credit rater to give them the best opinion they can about what the credit quality is of the security.

Unfortunately, that model does not seem to work. The problem is what economists call a free-rider problem. Basically, if five investors get together and pay Standard and Poor's to rate a particular issuance, unless they can keep that completely secret, anybody else can find out what the rating was and take advantage of that without being part of the consortium that paid.

So there have been a lot of ideas out there about how you can restructure the payment system to create better incentives for credit raters. But it is a challenging problem because, again, the "obvious solution" of having the investors pay only works if the investors collectively can share the cost and somehow keep that information from being spread among other investors.

The Aftermath of the Crisis

Today I want to talk about the aftermath of the crisis. To recap, I talked last time about the most intense phase of the crisis, in late 2008 and early 2009: financial panic both in United States and in other industrialized countries; the threat to the stability of the entire global financial system; the Federal Reserve in its lender of last resort role, working with others, provided short-term liquidity to help stabilize key institutions and markets.

One of the conclusions we can now draw, having looked at the history, is that rather than being some ad hoc and unprecedented set of actions, the Fed's response was very much in keeping with the historic role of central banks, which is to provide lender of last resort facilities in order to calm a panic. What was different about this crisis was that the institutional structure was different. It was not banks and depositors; it was broker-dealers and repo markets, money market funds and commercial paper. But the basic idea of providing short-term liquidity in order to stem a panic was very much what Bagehot envisioned when he wrote *Lombard Street* in 1873.

I have been focusing on the Fed's actions, but the Fed did not work alone. We worked in close coordination with other U.S. authorities and foreign authorities. For example, the Treasury was engaged after the Congress approved the so-called TARP legislation. The Treasury was in charge of making sure that banks had sufficient capital and the U.S. government took an ownership position in many banks that was essentially temporary. Most of those have now been reversed. The FDIC played an important role. In particular, the $250,000 deposit insurance limits were raised essentially to infinity for transaction accounts. And the FDIC also provided guarantees to banks that wanted to issue corporate paper of up to three years' maturity in the marketplace. For a fee, the FDIC guaranteed those issuances so that banks could get longer-term funding. So this was a collaborative effort between the Fed and other U.S. agencies.

We also worked closely with foreign agencies. I mentioned last time the currency swaps, in which the Fed gave dollars to foreign central banks in exchange for their own currencies. And those foreign central banks took the dollars and, at their own risk, made dollar loans to financial institutions that required dollar funding. We also, of course, continue to be in close touch with finance ministers and regulators around the world as we try to coordinate to deal with the crisis.

Putting out the most intense phase of the fire was not really enough. There has been a continuing effort to strengthen the financial and banking systems. For example, in a quite successful action that I think was very constructive, the Fed, working with the other banking agencies, led stress tests of the nineteen largest U.S. banks in the spring of 2009. This was not long after the most intense phase of the crisis. In an unprecedented way, we disclosed to the markets what the financial positions were of the major banks. Those stress tests, which confirmed that our banks could survive even a return to worse economic and financial conditions, created a great deal of confidence in investors and allowed banks to raise a great deal of private capital and, in many cases, to replace the government capital they received during the crisis. The process of stress testing has continued. Just a couple of weeks ago, the Fed led another round of stress tests, a very demanding set of stress tests. Our banks did quite well. They have raised a great deal of capital even since 2009. In many ways, they are in a stronger position in terms of capital than they were even prior to the crisis.

So these are steps that are being taken to try to get the banks back into full lending mode. It is still in progress, but restoring the integrity and the effectiveness of the financial system is obviously part of getting us back to a more normal economic situation.

Let me say a few words about the lender of last resort programs. As I have already argued at some length, the programs did appear to be effective. They arrested runs on various types of financial institutions and they restored financial market functioning. The programs, which were instituted primarily in the fall of 2008, were mostly phased out by March 2010. And they were phased out really in two different ways.

First, some of the programs just came to an end. But more often, in making loans to provide liquidity to financial institutions, the Fed would charge an interest rate that was lower than the crisis rate, the panic rate, but higher than normal interest rates. And so as the financial system calmed down and rates came back down to more normal levels, it was no longer economically or financially attractive for the institutions to keep borrowing from the Fed, and so the program wound down quite naturally. We did not have to shut them down; they basically disappeared on their own.

The financial risks that the Federal Reserve took in the lender of last resort programs were quite minimal. As I have described, lending was mostly short term. It was backed by collateral in most cases. In December 2010, we reported to Congress all the details involved in twenty-one thousand loans that the Fed made during the crisis. Of those twenty-one thousand loans, zero defaulted. Every single one was paid back. So even though the objective of the program was stabilizing the system rather than profit making, the taxpayers did come out ahead on those loans.

So that was lender of last resort activity. That was the fire hose to put out the fire of the financial crisis. But even though the crisis was contained, the impact on the U.S. and global economies was severe. And new actions were needed to help the economy recover. Remembering that the two basic tools of central banks are lender of last resort policy and monetary policy, we now turn to the second tool, monetary policy, which was the primary tool used to try to bring the economy back after the trauma of the financial crisis.

Conventional monetary policy involves management of the overnight interest rate called the federal funds rate. By raising and lowering the short-term interest rate, the Fed can influence a broader range of interest rates. That, in turn, affects consumer spending, purchases of homes, capital investment by firms, and the like, and that provides demand for the output of the economy and can help stimulate a return to growth.

Just a few words on the institutional aspects. Monetary policy is conducted by the Federal Open Market Committee, which meets in Washington eight times a year. During the crisis, it sometimes also held video conferences. When we have a meeting of the FOMC, there are nineteen people sitting around the table. There are the seven members of the Board of Governors, who are appointed by the president and confirmed by the Senate. And then there are the twelve presidents of the twelve Federal Reserve banks, each of whom is appointed by the board of directors of that regional Reserve Bank and then confirmed by the Board of Governors in Washington. So there are nineteen people around the table. We all participate in the monetary policy discussion.

When it comes time to vote, the system is a little bit more complicated. At any given meeting only twelve people are able to vote. The seven members of the Board of Governors have a permanent vote at every meeting. The president of the New York Federal Reserve Bank also has a permanent vote, which goes back to the beginning

Percent

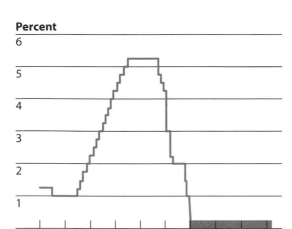

Figure 30. Federal Funds
Target Rate, 2003–2011
Source: Federal Reserve Board

of the system and the fact that New York remains the financial capital of the United States. For the other four votes, there is a rotation system: each year, four of the eleven other Reserve Bank presidents vote, and then the next year, a different set of four vote. So again, there is a total of twelve votes in any given meeting or on any given decision on monetary policy but the entire group participates in the discussions.

Figure 30 shows the federal funds rate, the short-term interest rate that is a normal tool the Fed uses for monetary policy. You can see that at the end of Chairman Greenspan's term and the beginning of my term in 2006, we were in the process of raising the federal funds rate in an attempt to normalize monetary policy after having easier policy earlier in the decade in order to help the economy recover from the 2001 recession. But in 2007, as problems began to appear in the subprime mortgage market, the Fed began to cut interest rates. You can see on the right side of the graph that interest rates were sharply reduced. And by December 2008, the federal funds rate was reduced to a range of between 0 and 25 basis points. A basis point is one-hundredth of 1 percent, so 25 basis points means one-quarter of 1 percent. By December 2008, the federal funds rate was reduced basically to zero. It cannot be cut any more, obviously.

So, as of December 2008, conventional monetary policy was exhausted. We could not cut the federal funds rate any further. And yet, the economy clearly needed additional support. Into 2009, the economy was still contracting at a rapid rate. We needed something else to support recovery, and so we turned to less conventional monetary policy. The main tool we have used is what we in the Fed call the large-scale asset purchases, or LSAPs, known in the press and elsewhere as quantitative easing, or QE. These large-scale asset purchases were an alternative way of easing monetary policy to provide support to the economy.

So how does this work? To influence longer-term rates, the Fed began to undertake large-scale purchases of Treasury and GSE mortgage-related securities. So, just to be clear here, the securities that the Fed has been purchasing are government-guaranteed securities, either Treasury securities, that is, government debt of the United States, or Fannie and Freddie securities, which were guaranteed by the U.S. government after Fannie and Freddie were taken into conservatorship.

There have been two major rounds of large-scale asset purchases, one announced in March 2009, often known as QE1, and another announced in November 2010, known as QE2. There have been some additional variations since then, including a program to lengthen the maturity of our existing assets, but these were the two biggest programs in terms of their size and their impact on the Fed's balance sheet. Taken together, these actions increased the Fed's balance sheet by more than two trillion dollars.

Figure 31 shows the asset side of the Fed's balance sheet, to help us see the effects of the large-scale asset purchases. The bottom layer is the traditional securities holdings. To be absolutely clear, even under normal circumstances the Fed always owns a substan-

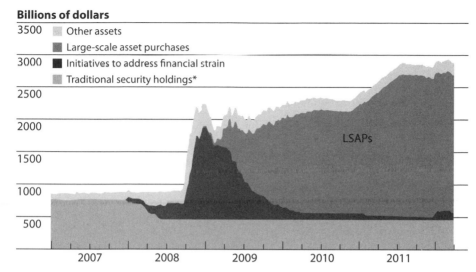

Billions of dollars

Figure 31. Federal Reserve Balance Sheet, Assets, 2007–2011
*Traditional security holdings reflect Treasury holdings through November 28, 2008; they are held constant after November 28, 2008.
Source: Federal Reserve Board

tial amount of U.S. Treasuries. We owned more than eight hundred billion dollars' worth of U.S. Treasuries before the crisis began. It is not as though we began buying them from scratch. We have always owned a significant amount of these securities. So the bottom layer shows the baseline from which we started.

What else appeared on the Fed's balance sheet on the assets side during this period? The dark segment just above the traditional securities holdings represents assets acquired or loans made during the crisis period. You can see that in late 2008, our loans outstanding to financial institutions and to some other programs rose very sharply. But you can also see that as time passed, and certainly by early 2010, those initiatives to address financial strength had been greatly reduced.

If you look at the far right, you see a little bump recently. That is the currency swaps. We instituted and extended swap agreements with the European Central Bank and other major central banks, and there has been some usage of that in an attempt to try to reduce strains in Europe, and that shows up as a little bump there at the far right of the graph. Now again, we owned about eight hundred billion dollars in Treasury securities at the beginning of the crisis. But as you can see from the large area labeled "LSAPs," we added about two trillion dollars in new securities to the balance sheet during the period starting in early 2009. And then at the top, you have other assets, a variety of things, security reserves, physical assets, and other miscellaneous items.

Why were we buying these securities? This is, by the way, an approach that monetarists such as Milton Friedman and others have talked about. The basic idea is that when you buy Treasuries or GSE securities and bring them onto the balance sheet, that reduces the available supply of those securities in the market. Investors want to hold those securities and they have to settle for a lower yield. Or, put another way, if there is a smaller available supply of those securities in the market, investors are willing to pay a higher price for those securities, which is the inverse of the yield.

So by purchasing Treasury securities, bringing them onto our balance sheet, and reducing the available supply of those Treasuries, we effectively lowered the interest rate of longer-termed Treasuries and GSE securities as well. Moreover, to the extent that investors no longer having available Treasuries and GSE securities to hold in their portfolios, to the extent that they are induced to move to other kinds of securities, such as corporate bonds, that also raises the prices and lowers the yields on those securities. And so the net effect of these actions was to lower yields across a range of securities. And as usual, lower interest rates have supportive, stimulative effects on the economy.

So this was really a monetary policy by another name: instead of focusing on the short-term rate, we were focusing on longer-term

Billions of dollars

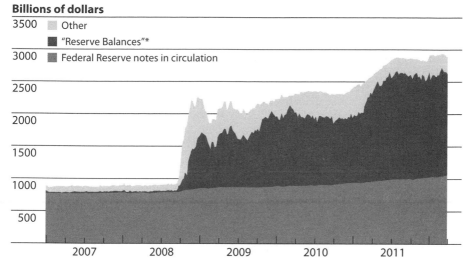

Figure 32. Federal Reserve Balance Sheet, Liabilities and Capital, 2007–2011
*Term deposits and other deposits held by depository institutions
Source: Federal Reserve Board

rates. But the basic logic of lowering rates to stimulate the economy is really the same.

You might ask, "The Fed is buying two trillion dollars' worth of securities. How do we pay for that?" The answer is that we paid for those securities by crediting the bank accounts of the people who sold them to us. And those accounts at the banks showed up as reserves that the banks would hold with the Fed. So the Fed is a bank for the banks. Banks can hold deposit accounts with the Fed, essentially, and those are called reserve accounts. And so as the purchases of securities occurred, the way we paid for them was basically by increasing the amount of reserves that banks had in their accounts with the Fed.

Figure 32 shows the liability side of the Fed's balance sheet. Of course, assets and liabilities including capital have to be equal. So the liability side had to rise to nearly three trillion dollars, as you can see. As you look at this, look first at the bottom layer, which is currency, Federal Reserve notes in circulation. Sometimes you hear that the Fed is printing money in order to pay for the securities we acquire. But as a literal fact, the Fed is not printing money to acquire the securities. And you could see it from the balance sheet here. That layer is basically flat; the amount of currency in circulation has not been affected by these activities.

What has been affected is the layer above that, reserve balances. Those are the accounts that commercial banks hold with the Fed, assets to the banking system and liabilities to the Fed, and that is basically how we pay for those securities. The banking system has a large quantity of these reserves, but they are electronic entries at the Fed. They basically just sit there. They are not in circulation. They are not part of any broad measure of the money supply. They are part of what is called the monetary base, but they certainly are not cash. Then the top layer is other liabilities, including Treasury accounts and a variety of other things that the Fed does. We act as the fiscal agent for the Treasury. But the two main items you can see are the notes in circulation and the reserves held by the banks.

So what do the LSAPs or the quantitative easing, what does it do? We anticipated when we took these actions that we would be able to lower interest rates, and that was generally successful. For example, thirty-year mortgage rates have fallen below 4 percent, which is a historically low level, but other interest rates have fallen as well. The interest rates corporations have to pay on bonds, for example, have fallen, both because the underlying safe rates have fallen but also because the spreads between corporate bond rates and Treasury rates have fallen as well, reflecting greater confidence in the financial markets about the economy. And lower long-term rates, in my view and in the Fed's analysis, have promoted growth and recovery.

Nonetheless, the effect on housing has been weaker than we hoped. We have gotten mortgage rates down very low. You would think that would stimulate housing, but the housing market has not yet recovered.

The Fed has a dual mandate; we always have two objectives. One of them is maximum employment, which we interpret to mean trying to keep the economy growing and using its full capacity, and low interest rates are a way of stimulating growth and trying to get people back to work. The second part of our mandate is price stability, low inflation. We have been quite successful in keeping inflation low. It has been a help that Volcker, in particular, and also Greenspan made it much easier for me because they had already persuaded markets that the Fed was committed to low inflation, and the Fed has built up a lot of credibility over the past thirty years or so. As a result, markets have been confident that the Fed will keep inflation low; inflation expectations have stayed low. And except for some swings up and down related to oil prices, overall, inflation has been quite low and stable.

At the same time, while we have kept inflation low, we have also made sure that inflation has not gone negative. Particularly around the time of QE2, in November 2010, there was concern that inflation had been falling. It was well below normal levels. The concern was we might get into negative inflation or deflation. Deflation has been a big problem for Japan's economy now for quite a few years, and I talked about deflation also in the context of the Great Depression. We certainly wanted to avoid deflation. So monetary ease also guarded against the risk of deflation by making sure that the economy did not get too weak.

One more comment on large-scale asset purchases. A lot of people do not distinguish between monetary and fiscal policy. Fiscal policy is the spending and taxation tools of the federal government. Monetary policy has to do with the Fed's management of interest rates. These are very different tools. And in particular, when the Fed buys assets as part of an LSAP or QE program, this is not a form of government spending. It does not show up as government spending because we are not actually spending money. What we are doing is buying assets, which at some point will be sold back to the market, and so the value of those purchases will be earned back. In fact, because the Fed gets interest on the securities we hold, we actually make a very nice profit on these LSAPs. What we have done over the past three years is transfer about two hundred billion dollars in profits to the Treasury. That money goes directly to reducing the deficit. So these actions are not deficit-increasing; they are in fact significantly deficit-reducing.

So a major tool we used when we ran out of room to lower short-term interest rates was LSAPs, asset purchases. The other tool we have used to some extent is communication about monetary policy. To the extent that we can clearly communicate what we are trying to achieve, investors can better understand our objectives and our plans, and that can make monetary policy more effective. The Fed has taken a lot of steps to become more transparent about monetary policy to try to make sure people understand what we are trying to accomplish.

For example, four times a year, after two-day FOMC meetings, I give a press conference and answer questions about monetary policy decisions. This is a new thing for the Fed in terms of trying to explain what our policies are.

Another recent step that we took in communicating our policies more clearly was to put out a statement that described our basic approach to monetary policy and, in particular, for the first time gave a numerical definition of price stability. Many central banks around the world already have a numerical definition of price stability, and in our statement we said that, for our purposes, we were going to define price stability as 2 percent inflation. And so, the markets will know that over the medium term, the Fed will try to hit 2 percent inflation, even as it also tries to hit its objectives for growth and employment.

Finally, the Fed has also begun to provide guidance to investors and the public about what we expect to do with the federal funds rate in the future, given how we currently see the economy. So, given how we currently see the economy, we tell the market something about where we think the rates are going to go. To the extent that the market better understands our plans, that is going to help reduce uncertainty in financial markets. And to the extent that our plans are, in some sense, more aggressive than the market anticipated, we will also tend to ease policy conditions.

The recession—the period of contraction, which was very severe—officially came to an end. There is a committee called the National Bureau of Economic Research, which officially designates the beginning and end dates of recessions. I was a member of that committee before I became a policymaker. And they determined that this recession began in December 2007 and ended in June 2009, so it was a long recession. When they say the recession ended, what that means basically is not that things are back to normal; it just means that the contraction has stopped and the economy is now growing again. So we have been growing now for almost three years, averaging about 2.5 percent a year. But as I described, we are still some distance from being back to normal. So when we say the economy is no longer in recession, we do not mean that things are great. We just mean that we are no longer actually contracting; we are now growing.

Figure 33 gives a picture of the sluggish economic recovery. The darker line in the graph shows the path of real GDP since 2007. The shaded area shows the period of the recession according to the National Bureau of Economic Research. You can see that it begins in December 2007, and real GDP begins to decline during that period.

Billions of chained (2005) dollars

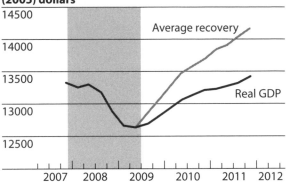

Figure 33. Real GDP, 2007–2012
Note: Vertical shading represents NBER recession dates. The average recovery is calculated using the average growth rate in quarters following NBER troughs since 1949.
Source: Bureau of Economic Analysis

In mid-2009, the recession is officially over. And you can see that, since then, the darker line has been moving up as the real economy has been expanding.

But you can also see a comparison. Suppose that the economy had been recovering since mid-2009 at the average pace of previous recoveries in the postwar period. That average recovery is shown by the lighter line. You can see that this recovery has been slower than the average recovery in the post–World War II period. It is actually even worse than that, in a way, because this was the most severe recession in the post–World War II period. And so you would expect that recovery might be a little quicker as the economy comes back to its normal level, but in fact it has been actually slower in terms of growth than previous postwar recoveries.

An implication of the sluggish recovery is only very slow improvement in the unemployment rate. In figure 34, you can see the unemployment rate rising sharply during the recession period, peaking at around 10 percent, and then slowly coming down to its current value of about 8.3 percent. That is still quite high. Figure 35 shows single-family housing starts. As I discussed, housing starts collapsed even before the recession began. Of course, that was a trigger of the recession. And you see how very sharply construction

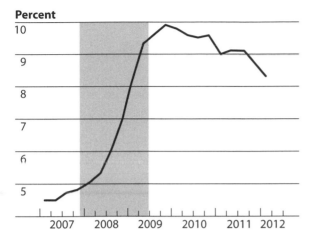

Percent

Figure 34. Unemployment
Rate, 2007–2012
Note: Vertical shading represents
NBER recession dates. Value of
the first quarter of 2012 is the
February reading.
Source: Bureau of Labor
Statistics

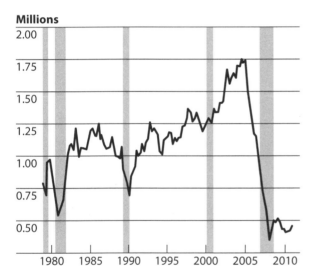

Millions

Figure 35. Single-Family
Housing Starts, 1979–2011
Note: Vertical shading represents
NBER recession dates.
Source: Census Bureau

declined. If you look at the most recent year or two, you see that
there have been a few little wiggles, but the housing market has not
come back.

So this is one answer to the question, why has this recovery been
more sluggish than normal? One reason certainly is the housing
market. In a usual recovery, housing comes back. It is an important

**Percent of
housing units** (quarterly)

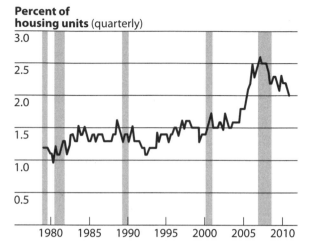

Figure 36. Homeowner Vacancy Rate for Single-Family Homes, 1980–2010
Note: Vertical shading represents NBER recession dates.
Source: Census Bureau

part of the recovery process. Construction workers get put back to work, related industries such as furniture and appliances begin to expand, and that is part of the recovery process. But in this case, we have not seen that. Why not?

There are still a lot of structural factors in the housing market that are preventing a more robust recovery. On the supply side, we still have a very high excess supply of housing, a high vacancy rate. Figure 36 shows the percentage of housing units in the United States that are vacant, such as foreclosed homes or homes where the seller is unable to find a buyer. You can see that the vacancy rate peaked at more than 2.5 percent during the recession. It has come down some but is still well above normal levels. There are a lot of homes on the market, and that produces excess supply and falling house prices.

On the demand side, you might think that a lot of people would be buying houses these days because houses are really affordable. Prices are down a lot; mortgage rates are low. And so if you are able to buy a house, you can get an awful lot of house for your monthly payment now, compared to a few years ago. But being able to take advantage of that affordability requires, among other things, that

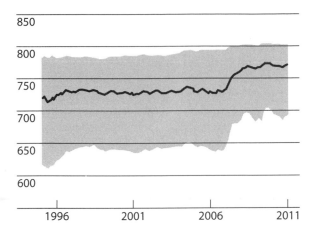

Figure 37. Credit Scores on Newly Originated Mortgages, 1995–2011
Note: Shaded region shows tenth to ninetieth percentile; line shows the median.
Source: LPS Applied Analytics

you get a mortgage. Figure 37 shows what is happening in the mortgage market. The bottom line shows the tenth percentile and the top line the ninetieth percentile of credit scores of people receiving mortgages. And you can see that before the crisis, people with relatively low credit scores were able to get mortgages. But since the crisis, you can see the whole bottom part of the shaded area has been cut away, implying that people with lower credit scores—and 700 is not a terrible credit score—are unable to get mortgages. In general, conditions have been much tighter for obtaining mortgages. So even though housing is very affordable and monthly payments are affordable, a lot of people are unable to get mortgages.

So, with a lot of excess supply in the housing market and with a lot of people unable to get mortgage credit or afraid to get back into the housing market, house prices have been declining, as shown in figure 38. Recently we have seen some leveling off, but so far not much evidence of an upturn. Declining house prices mean it is not profitable to build new houses, and so construction has been quite weak. And more broadly, when existing homeowners see their house prices decline, it may mean they cannot get home equity lines of credit or they just feel poorer. And so that affects not just their housing behavior, but also their willingness and ability to buy other

Index, Jan. 2000 = 100

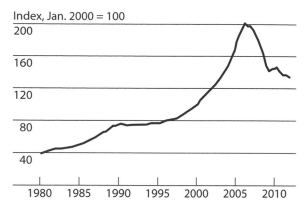

Figure 38. Prices of Existing Single-Family Houses,
1980–2012
Note: Includes purchase transactions only.
Source: CoreLogic

business services. So the declines in housing prices and, to some extent, also stock prices are part of the reason consumers have been cautious and less willing to spend.

Housing was a major cause of this crisis and recession. The other major factor was the financial crisis and its impact on credit markets. And that is another reason the recovery has been somewhat slower than we would have hoped. As I have discussed, the U.S. banking system is stronger than it was three years ago. The amount of capital in the banking system over the past three years has increased by something like three hundred billion dollars, a very significant increase. And generally speaking, we are seeing credit terms getting a bit easier. We are seeing expansions in bank lending in a lot of categories. So there is certainly some improvement in banking and credit.

Nevertheless, there are still scenarios where credit remains tight. I have already talked about mortgages: if you have anything less than a perfect credit score, it is very difficult to get a mortgage these days. And other categories such as small businesses have also found it difficult to get credit. It is well known that small business is an important creator of jobs, so the inability to start a small business or to get credit to expand a small business is one of the reasons job creation has been relatively slow.

Another aspect of financial and credit markets has to do with the European situation. Following the financial crisis in Europe, which was very severe alongside of ours, there is now a second stage in which the solvency issues of a number of countries, the concerns about whether countries such as Greece and Portugal and Ireland can pay their creditors, have led to stressed financial conditions in Europe. And those have negatively affected the United States by creating risk aversion and volatility in the financial markets.

A lesson worth drawing from this is that monetary policy is a powerful tool but it cannot solve all the problems that there are. And in particular, what we are seeing in this recovery is a number of structural issues relating, for example, to the housing market, to the mortgage market, to banks, to credit extension, and of course to the European situation, where other kinds of policies—whether fiscal policies or housing policies or whatever they may be—are needed to get the economy going again. So the Fed can provide stimulus. It can provide low interest rates. But monetary policy by itself cannot solve important structural, fiscal, and other problems that affect the economy.

This is all rather discouraging. Again, it has taken a while to get back to where we are, and we are still a long way from where we would like to be. So let me say a few words about the long run. We did have, of course, a major trauma. The crisis was very deep. We have a lot of people who have been unemployed for a long time. About 40 percent or more of all the unemployed had been unemployed for six months or more. And if you are unemployed for six months or a year or two years, your skills will start to atrophy and your ability to get reemployed will decline. So that clearly is a problem. And then there are many other issues that the United States was facing even before the crisis, such as federal budget deficits, and those have not gone away. In fact, they have gotten somewhat worse through the recession. So clearly, there have been some real headwinds for our economy.

That said, I think it is important to understand that our economy has faced many short-term shocks in the past, and some not so short-term, but it has always been able to recover. We have a lot of strengths in this economy. It is, of course, the largest economy in the world; between 20 and 25 percent of all output in the world is produced in the United States, even though we have something like 6 percent or less of the world's population. And the reason that we are so productive has to do with the diverse set of industries we have; our entrepreneurial culture, which still is clearly the best in the world; the flexibility of our labor markets and our capital markets; and our technology, which remains one of our very strongest points. Increasingly, technology has been driving economic growth. And with some of the finest universities and research centers in the world as magnets for talented people from around the world, the United States has been very successful in the research and development area. So, that has also been a source of ongoing growth and innovation in our economy. Again, we have weaknesses and the financial crisis highlighted a few, but we have also tried to address them by strengthening our financial regulatory system.

I find figure 39 interesting, to put in perspective what I have been discussing during these lectures. The dashed line shows a constant growth rate of a little over 3 percent in real terms. This is a log scale, so the straight line means a constant growth rate. And you can see that, going back to 1900, the United States economy has grown reasonably consistently at around 3 percent annually for more than a century. In the 1930s, you can see the big swing as the Great Depression pulled actual output below the trend line. And then you can see the movement above the trend line during World War II. But look what happened after World War II: we went right back to the trend line. There were recessions and booms and busts in the postwar period, but growth remained fairly close to the trend line. Now, if you look to the very far right, you see where we are today: we are below the trend line. There are debates about whether that de-

Billions of chained (2005) dollars, log scale

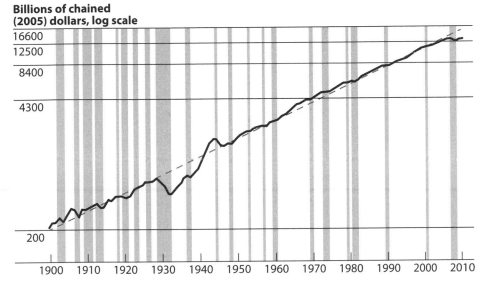

Figure 39. Real GDP, 1900–2010
Note: Vertical shading represents NBER recession dates; dashed line denotes trend.
Sources: For 1900–1928, Historical Statistics of the United States, Millennial Edition, table Ca9; for 1929–present, Bureau of Economic Analysis

cline is permanent. But looking at history, I think there is a reasonable chance that the U.S. economy will return to a healthy annual growth rate somewhere in the 3 percent range. There are factors to take into account, such as changes in our population growth rate, the aging of our population, and so on. But broadly speaking, what this graph shows is that, over long periods, our economy has been successful in maintaining long-term economic growth.

I will say a few words about regulatory changes. In the last couple of lectures I discussed the vulnerabilities in both the private and public sectors in the financial system. On the public side, the crisis revealed many weaknesses in our regulatory system. We saw what happened with Lehman Brothers and AIG, the effects of the "too big to fail" problem on our system, and more generally, the problem of the lack of attention to the broad stability of the system as opposed to individual parts of the system.

There has been a very substantial amount of financial regulatory reform in the United States since 2008, and the biggest piece of legislation is the so-called Dodd-Frank Act.[5] This legislation, officially named the Wall Street Reform and Consumer Protection Act, which was passed in the summer of 2010, was a comprehensive set of financial reforms addressing many of the vulnerabilities that I discussed earlier.

Now, what were these vulnerabilities? One was the fact that there was nobody watching over the whole system, nobody looking at the entire financial system to spot risks and threats to overall financial stability. So, one of the main themes of the Dodd-Frank Act is to try to create a systemic approach, where regulators look at the whole system and not just individual components of it. Among the tools to do that is a newly created council called the Financial Stability Oversight Council (FSOC), of which the Fed is a member, which helps regulators coordinate. We meet regularly in this council and discuss economic and financial developments and talk about ways that we can look at the whole system and try to avoid various kinds of problems.

Moreover, the Dodd-Frank Act gave all regulators responsibility to take into account broad systemic implications of their own individual regulatory and supervisory actions. And in particular, the Federal Reserve has greatly restructured our supervisory divisions so that we are looking now very comprehensively at a whole range of financial markets and financial institutions. As a result, now we have a big picture that we did not have before the crisis.

I mentioned in my discussion of vulnerabilities the many gaps in the financial system. There were important firms, such as AIG, for

---

[5] In United States, legislation is unofficially named after the chairs of the relevant committees. Barney Frank was the chairman of the House Financial Services Committee when the Democrats controlled the House in 2010, and Chris Dodd was the chairman of the Senate Banking Committee.

example, but others as well, that had no significant comprehensive oversight by any regulatory agency. The Dodd-Frank Act provides a fail-safe in that the FSOC can designate, by vote, any institution it views as not being adequately regulated to come under the supervision of the Federal Reserve. That process is going on now. So there will not be any more large, complex, systemically critical firms that have no oversight. Likewise, the FSOC can also designate the so-called financial market utilities like a stock exchange or some other major exchange to be supervised by the Fed and other agencies. So those gaps are being closed. We will not have the situation that we had before the crisis.

Another set of problems had to do with "too big to fail" and dealing with firms that are systemically critical. The approach to dealing with too big to fail or systemically critical institutions is two-pronged. On the one hand, under Dodd-Frank, large, complex, systemically important financial institutions are going to face tougher supervision regulation than other firms. The Federal Reserve, working with international regulators, has established higher capital requirements that these firms will be subject to, including surcharges for the very largest and most systemic firms. Rules like the Volcker Rule, which prohibits bank affiliates from taking risky bets on their own accounts, will try to reduce the riskiness of large firms. Stress tests will be conducted. Dodd-Frank requires that large firms be stress tested by the Fed once a year and conduct their own stress tests once a year. So we will be comfortable, or at least more comfortable, that these firms can withstand a major shock to the financial system.

Now, one part of tackling "too big to fail" is to bring these large, complex firms under more stringent scrutiny: more supervision, more capital reserves, more stress tests, more restrictions on their activities. But the other side of tackling "too big to fail" is, well, failing. In the crisis, the Fed and the other financial agencies faced a terrible choice of either trying to prevent some large firms such as AIG from failing, which was a bad choice because it ratified "too big to fail" and meant that the firms were not adequately punished for the risks they took, or letting them fail and potentially destabilize the whole financial system and the economy. So that is the "too big to fail" problem. The only way to solve that problem, in the end, is to make it safe for a big firm to fail. One of the main elements of the Dodd-Frank Act is what is called the "orderly liquidation authority," which has been given to the FDIC. The FDIC already has the authority to shut down a failing bank, and it can do that quickly and efficiently, typically over the weekend. And depositors are made whole. The FDIC's ability to do that has prevented panics and bank runs since the 1930s. The idea here is that the FDIC will do something similar, but for large, complex firms, which obviously is much more difficult. But in cooperation with the Fed, and with regulators from other countries in the case of multinational firms, work is under way to prepare. So should it happen that a large firm comes to the brink of insolvency and cannot find a solution—cannot find new capital, for example—the Fed's ability to intervene the way we did in 2008 has been taken away. Legally, we cannot do that anymore. The only option we will have is to work with the FDIC to safely wind down the firm, and that will ultimately reduce or, we hope, eliminate the "too big to fail" problem.

There are many other aspects of the Dodd-Frank Act. Another vulnerability I discussed was the exotic financial instruments, derivatives and so on, that concentrated risk. There is a whole set of new rules that require more transparency about derivatives positions, standardization of derivatives, and trading of derivatives through third parties called central counterparties. The idea here is to take derivatives and those transactions out of the shadows, to make them available and visible to both the regulators and the markets to avoid a situation like we saw during the crisis.

The Federal Reserve did not do as good a job as it should have in protecting consumers on the mortgage front. So the Dodd-Frank Act creates a new agency, called the Consumer Financial Protection Bureau, which is meant to protect consumers in their financial dealings, and that would include things like protections on the terms of mortgages, for example.

So there is quite a variety of aspects of Dodd-Frank. It is a large and complex bill, and there has been a lot of complaining about the fact that it is large and complex. The regulators are doing their best to implement these rules in a way that will be effective and, at the same time, minimize the cost to the industry and to the economy. That is difficult, but it is an ongoing process. We do that through an extensive process of putting out proposed rules, gathering comments from the public, looking at those comments, making changes to the rules, and so on. It is an iterative process through which we put in place these regulatory standards. And again, it is still very much under way.

Let me conclude by saying a couple of things about the future. Central banks, not just in the United States but around the world, have been through a very difficult and dramatic period, which has required a lot of rethinking about how we manage policy and how we manage our responsibilities with respect to the financial system. In particular, during much of the World War II period, because things were relatively stable, because financial crises were things that happened in emerging markets and not in developed countries, many central banks began to view financial stability policy as a junior partner to monetary policy. It was not considered as important. It was something to which they paid attention, but it was not something to which they devoted many resources.

Obviously, based on what happened during the crisis and the effects we are still feeling, it is now clear that maintaining financial stability is just as important a responsibility as maintaining monetary and economic stability. And indeed, this is a return to where the Fed came from in the beginning. Remember that the reason that Fed was created was to try to reduce the incidence of financial panics; financial stability was the original goal in creating the Fed. So now we have come full circle.

Financial crises will always be with us. That is probably unavoidable. We have had financial crises for six hundred years in the Western world. Periodically, there are going to be bubbles or other instabilities in the financial system. But given what the potential for damage is now, as we have seen, it is really important for central banks and other regulators to do what we can, first, to anticipate or prevent a crisis, but also, if a crisis happens, to mitigate it and to make sure the system is strong enough to make it through the crisis intact.

Again, we began by noting the two principle tools of central banks, serving as lender of last resort to prevent or mitigate financial crises, and using monetary policy to enhance economic stability. In the Great Depression, as I described, those tools were not used appropriately. But in the recent episode, the Fed and other central banks used these tools actively. I should also say that there has been a great convergence, that other major central banks have followed policies very similar to that of the Fed. And in any case, I believe that by using these tools actively, we avoided much worse outcomes in terms of both the financial crisis and the depth and severity of the resulting recession. A new regulatory framework will be helpful. But again, it is not going to solve the problem. The only solution in the end is for us regulators and our successors to continue to monitor the entire financial system and to try to identify problems and to respond to them using the tools that we have.

STUDENT: In the first lecture, you touched on the Main Street versus Wall Street divide, and this has been in the back of my mind throughout the lecture series. You have talked about the importance of educating the public on monetary policy. And although this lecture series has definitely demystified the Fed for me, I think it has really been Wall Street, not Main Street, that has been tuning in. So, given how unpopular bank bailouts were among many Americans struggling to pay their mortgages who don't really understand the importance of financial stability, do you ever see Americans reconciling these differences?

CHAIRMAN BERNANKE: You're right. Some of the same conflicts that we saw in the nineteenth century, we see echoes of them today as well. I do not have a simple answer to that question. As you know, the Fed has done more outreach—the press conferences and other kinds of tools—to try to explain what we did and what we are doing. Clearly, the Fed is very accountable. We testify frequently, not just myself but other members of the Board or Reserve Bank presidents. We give speeches. We appear at various events and so on.

It is inherently difficult because the Fed is a complicated institution. And as you have seen in these four lectures, these are not simple issues. But all we can do, I think, is to do our best and hope that our educators, our media, and so on will begin to carry the story and help people understand better. It is a difficult challenge and it does reflect a tension in American feelings about central banks ever since the beginning.

STUDENT: Earlier you mentioned that the Fed had several ways to unwind the large-scale asset purchases, including selling them back into the market. What guarantees that investors will be willing to buy them back in the future?

CHAIRMAN BERNANKE: We have essentially three separate types of tools that we can use, any one of which by itself would allow us to unwind our policies. But taken together, they give us a lot of comfort.

First, we have the ability to pay interest on the reserves that banks hold with us. So, when the time comes for the Fed to raise interest rates, we can do so by raising the rate of interest we pay to banks on those reserves. Banks are not going to lend out the reserves at a rate lower than they can earn at the Fed. And so that will lock up those reserves, raise interest rates, and serve to tighten monetary policy. So, that one tool by itself, even if our balance sheets stayed large, could tighten monetary policy.

The second tool we have is what are called draining tools. Basically, we have various ways that we can drain the reserves from the banking system and replace them with other kinds of liabilities even as the total amount of assets on our balance sheet remains unchanged.

The third and final option is either to let the assets run off as they mature or to sell them. These are Treasury securities and government-guaranteed securities. It is certainly possible that the prevailing interest rate when we sell those securities will be higher than it is today. In other words, we will have to pay a higher interest rate in order to make investors willing to acquire them. But actually, that will be part of the process. That will be a time when we are trying to raise interest rates. It will be the reverse of what we did when we bought them. At that point, we will be trying to raise interest rates in order to exit from the easy policy to a policy that will allow the economy to grow in a low-inflationary way.

So, I do not think there is any danger that investors will not buy the assets. They will certainly buy them at a higher interest rate, and that would be part of the objective of reducing the balance sheet to tighten financial conditions, so as to avoid inflation concerns in the future.

STUDENT: I read an article that laid out a plan to allow homeowners who have been on time with their mortgage payments to refinance at the current lower rates as a way to protect them from their housing prices dropping. I was wondering whether you have heard of plans like that and what sort of involvement the Fed would have or whether that would fall to the Consumer Financial Protection Bureau.

CHAIRMAN BERNANKE: There are some programs like that, one in particular is called the HARP program, which is run by the GSEs, Fannie and Freddie, and by their regulator, the Federal Housing Finance Agency. In this program, if you are underwater in your mortgage—in other words, if you owe more on your mortgage than your house is worth—you still may be able, under this program, if your mortgage is held by Fannie or Freddie, to refinance at a lower interest rate, which will reduce your payments. That program is under way and being expanded. It does not necessarily work if your mortgage is being held by a bank because they are not part of this program, but they may choose voluntarily to do it. But you might be out of luck if your mortgage is not held by Fannie or Freddie.

So, there are programs like that. The Fed is not involved in them. Our job has been to keep mortgage rates low and hope that we can help homeowners. But programs like that, which allow people to get lower payments, obviously are going to be helpful to those people because they will face less financial stress, and there would be a smaller chance that they will end up being delinquent on their mortgages.

STUDENT: You mentioned in your lecture the dangers of deflation from the Great Depression and more recently in Japan. And one of the arguments for maintaining a target inflation rate above zero is to provide a cushion against the possibility of deflation. Yet in the last two recessions in the United States, there has been a significant fear of deflation, causing the Fed to keep monetary policy very accommodative in the beginning of the last decade and even more so at this point. Do you think that 2 percent is enough of a cushion to prevent deflation? And have you considered higher inflation target rates?

CHAIRMAN BERNANKE: That is a great question, and there has been a lot of research on it. It seems that the international consensus is around 2 percent. Almost all central banks that have a target have either a 2 percent target or a 1–3 percent target or something similar. And there is a trade-off here, because, on the one hand, you want to have it above zero, as you say, in order to avoid or reduce deflation risk. But on the other hand, if inflation is too high, it is going to create problems for markets. It is going to make the economy less efficient. And so there is a trade-off in which one level of inflation gives you at least some reasonable buffer against deflation, but it is not so high that it makes markets work less well. And so again, the international consensus has been around 2 percent, and that is where the Fed has been informally for quite a while. So that is what we announced, and for the foreseeable future that is where we plan to stay. But obviously researchers will continue to look at this issue, trying to pinpoint exactly where the optimal trade-off is.

STUDENT: You mentioned that one of the biggest lessons you learned from the recent financial crisis is that monetary policy is powerful but it cannot solve all the problems, especially structural problems. What are the effective tools that can be used to solve these structural problems in housing and financial and credit markets?

CHAIRMAN BERNANKE: It depends on the particular set of problems. In the case of housing, the Federal Reserve staff wrote a white paper that analyzed a number of the issues, not just foreclosures, but also what to do with vacant houses, how to get more appropriate mortgage origination conditions, and issues of that sort. We did not come out with a list of actual recommendations because that is really up to Congress and to other agencies to determine. But we did go through a whole list of possible approaches.

But housing is a very complex problem, and there are many different things that could be done to try to make it work better. And indeed, looking forward, given the problems with Fannie and Freddie, we have some very big decisions to make as a country about what our housing finance system is going to look like in the longer term.

In Europe, for example, there has been a very complex problem. We have been in close discussions with our European colleagues. They have taken a number of steps. Right now they are talking about a so-called firewall, how much money they are going to contribute to provide protection against the possibility of contagion if some country defaults or fails to pay its bills.

Each of these issues has its own approach. In the labor market, we have the problem of people who have been out of work for a long time. Obviously, one of the best ways to deal with that would be some form of training, increasing skills. So you could just go down the list. And basically, anything that makes our economy more productive, more efficient, and deals with some of these long-term issues related to our fiscal problems, those are all things that would help. And the fact that the Fed is doing what we can to try to support the recovery should not mean that no other policies are undertaken. I think it is important that we look across the entire government and ask what kinds of constructive steps can be taken to make our economy stronger and to help the recovery be more sustainable.

STUDENT: You mentioned that the Fed is doing what it can to sustain the recovery, but with unemployment at 8.3 percent and the housing market very sluggish and the problems in Europe, what other tools does the Fed have to address other issues that might arise in the future—say, if unemployment starts to rise, or the housing recovery gets worse, or Portugal, Spain, and Italy default?

CHAIRMAN BERNANKE: Oh, my! You will cost me a night's sleep now. What I described today is basically what the toolkit is for the Federal Reserve and other central banks. We still have lender of last resort authority. It has been modified in some ways by the Dodd-Frank Act—strengthened in some ways and reduced in some ways. So between that and our financial regulatory authority, we want to make sure our financial system is strong. And we have worked particularly hard to make sure that we do everything we can to protect our financial system and our economy from anything that might happen in Europe. So, that whole set of tools is still available and in play should there be any new problems in financial markets.

On the monetary side, we do not have any completely new monetary tools, but we have our interest-rate policies, and we can continue to use monetary policy as appropriate as the outlook changes to try to achieve the appropriate recovery while still maintaining price stability, which is the other half of the Federal Reserve mandate.

So we have these two basic sets of tools. We will have to continue to evaluate where the economy is going and use them appropriately. We do not have lots of other tools. And that is why I was saying earlier that we really need an effort across different parts of the government, and indeed the private sector, to do what can be done to get our economy back on its feet.

STUDENT: You spoke a lot about the economic recovery and that, although it is painfully slow, there is a clear recovery happening. What are the key indicators that you and the Federal Reserve are looking at that would suggest that the private sector has begun self-sustaining this economic recovery and that the Fed may begin to tighten monetary policy?

CHAIRMAN BERNANKE: That is a great question. First, one set of indicators that has been looking better lately and we have been paying a lot of attention to is developments in the labor market, jobs, unemployment rate, unemployment insurance claims, hours of work, all of those indicators suggest that the labor market is strengthening. And indeed, employment is one of our two objectives. So clearly, that is something we would like to see sustained. We would like to see a continued improvement in the labor market.

As I discussed in the third lecture, it is much more likely that the improvement in the labor market will be sustained if we also see increases in overall demand and overall growth. So we will continue to look at indicators of consumer spending and consumer sentiment, capital plans, capital expenditures, indicators of optimism on the part of firms, those kinds of things, to see where production and demand are going to go. And then, of course, as always, we have to look at inflation and be comfortable that price stability will be maintained and that inflation will be low and stable. So those are the things we will be looking at, and there is no simple formula. But as the economy strengthens and becomes more self-sustaining, then at some point the need for so much support from the Fed will begin to diminish.

Index